Vishnu
The Eternal Preserver

YASHVI JALAN

BLUEROSE PUBLISHERS
India | U.K.

Copyright © Yashvi Jalan 2024

All rights reserved by author. No part of this publication may be reproduced, stored in a retrieval system or transmitted in any form or by any means, electronic, mechanical, photocopying, recording or otherwise, without the prior permission of the author. Although every precaution has been taken to verify the accuracy of the information contained herein, the publisher assumes no responsibility for any errors or omissions. No liability is assumed for damages that may result from the use of information contained within.

BlueRose Publishers takes no responsibility for any damages, losses, or liabilities that may arise from the use or misuse of the information, products, or services provided in this publication.

For permissions requests or inquiries regarding this publication, please contact:

BLUEROSE PUBLISHERS
www.BlueRoseONE.com
info@bluerosepublishers.com
+91 8882 898 898
+4407342408967

ISBN: 978-93-6452-800-9

Cover Design: Sadhna Kumari
Typesetting: Pooja Sharma

First Edition: September 2024

Contents

1. Introduction 1
2. The Beginning 9
3. Matsya Avatar 13
4. Kachhap Avatar 18
5. Varaha Avatar 23
6. Narsimha Avatar 26
7. Vamana Avatar 30
8. Parshuram Avatar 33
9. Ram Avatar 36
10. Krishna Avatar 61
11. Buddha Avatar 115
12. Kalki Avatar 121
13. Conclusion 122

1. Introduction

Prologue:

Yada yada hi dharmasya glanir bhavati bharata I

Abhyutthanam adharmasya tadatmanam srijamyaham II

Paritranaya sadhunam vinashaya cha dushkritam I

Dharma sansthapanarthaya sambhavami yuge yuge II

(Whenever there is decimation of righteousness and surge in wickedness, O descendant of Bharat, I manifest myself periodically to protect the righteous, to destroy the wicked, and to re-establish the dharma.)

Yuga:

Yuga is a cyclic age in Hindu cosmology. Scriptures state that each cycle lasts for 4,320,000 years. This cycle is divided into four stages each consisting of 12,000 divine years namely "Satya Yuga", "Treta Yuga" "Dvapara yuga" and "Kala Yuga". With the flow of time, dharma relinquishes from Satya Yuga to Kala

Yuga and adharma's grasp strengthens. Finally, when adharma is at its peak, it becomes necessary to destroy the world and create a new one. It is well said that the mechanism of these stages lies in the hands of the "Tridevas" (Vishnu, Brahma and Shiva). While Lord Brahma creates this cycle, Lord Shiva causes destruction during the end phase of Kala Yuga and opens a room for a new creation. Lord Vishnu takes frequent avatars to maintain an equilibrium in adharma and dharma. The consorts of the Tridevis, Lakshmi (Goddess of wealth), Saraswati (Goddess of Knowledge), Parvati/Shakti (Goddess of strength) equally assist their respective husbands in performing their duties. In each cycle, Lord Vishnu takes 10 incarnations namely, Matysa (Fish avatar), Kachhap (Tortoise avatar), Narsingh (Human-lion avatar), Varaha (Boar avatar), Vamana (Brahmin Avatar), Parshurama, Rama, Krishna, Gautam Buddha and Kalki. In every avatar of Lord Vishnu, his counterpart, Devi Lakshmi incarnates with him and portrays the fact that with the supreme power of love, any hurdle or obstacle lying in the path can be overcome. The sacrifice, humiliation, difficulties and pain of separation encountered by both Vishnu and Lakshmi for the welfare of the world is what makes them and their love eternal.

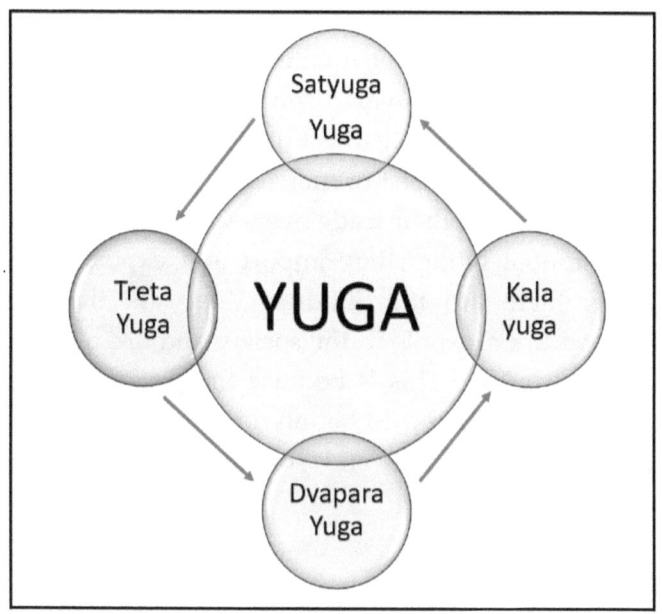

Structure of the Society:

The structure of the society throughout the book is following the federal system. In India it is also called caste system. This multi-dimensional hierarchy consists of Brahmins, Kshatriyas, Vaishyas and Shudras. The Brahmins are the one who are given the most amount of prestige. The fact that they gain access to qualified education is what gives them the highest rank in the Hindu Caste. They are said to have a direct connection with the omnipresent which makes them our messengers. In earlier times, they were recognized as eclectic people who transmitted the demand of the commoners to the almighty. Next are the Kshatriyas who mainly compromise of the kings, princes and nobilities. They are the rulers who protect people. Thus, they are given adequate amount of knowledge regarding weapons which can help them efficiently perform their duty. In the third place, we have the Vaishyas. They consist of merchants and traders who have established their trade overseas. In order to earn a substantial living, they import and export goods. Lastly, there are the Shudras. They are the most frowned upon people in the society and are regarded as untouchables. This is because the profession they opt for is considered to be inferior and classless. The commoners, peasants and servants fall under this category.

An Inter Relation:

"**Ardhang**" **and** "**Ardhangani**" are two inter related Sanskrit words which typically mean "Husband" and "Wife". However, when broken into two equal halves, "*ardh* means half while *ang* means body". Hence, our scriptures consider husband and wife to be each other's better half. The fact that husbands and wives are interdependent on each other and their existence is of no use without their respective consorts is also depicted in context to the Tridevas and Tridevis. Devi Lakshmi, the Goddess of wealth is wedded to Lord Narayan, the preserver. A closer glance accentuates the fact that in order for preservation to take place, wealth is required. Similarly, Lord Mahadev, the destructor and Devi Parvati, the Goddess of power are married to each other. In order for destruction to take place power is an utmost requirement. And lastly, Lord Brahma, the creator and Devi Saraswati, the Goddess of Knowledge are also married. And creation is impossible without knowledge. This extraordinary and beautiful connection verifies the saying that "Completeness of husbands and wives lie in each other."

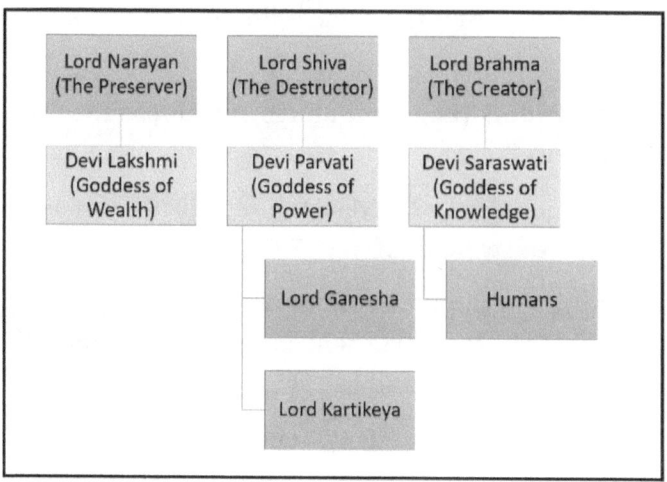

Weapons of Lord Narayan:

Lord Narayan is also known as **"Chaturbhuja"**, the one having four hands. Each of the four weapons possessed by Lord Narayan are eclectic in themselves. The significance and name of each of the **Astras** (weapons) are given below.

a. **The Shankha (conch)**: It represents him as the **"God of sound"**. This conch shell trumpet is blown to announce his presence on a battlefield. In Vedic times, this instrument was used by the commander to rally their troops. Every warrior had their very own conch shell. It was viewed as a symbol of **communication.**

b. **The Sudarshan Chakra**: It is one of the most powerful weapons in the world. It consists of 108 serrated blades and has the ability to travel several million yojanas (1 yojana = 8 kms) at a blink of an eye.

c. **The Padma (Lotus)**: It represents him as the **"God of peace"**.

d. **Kaumodaki Gada (Mace)**: It represents him as the **"God of strength"**.

Due to this a popular epithet of Vishnu is <u>*Shankha-Chakra-Gada-Pani*</u> (He who holds in his hands the conch, chakra, lotus and gada).

Vishnu's carrot and stick approach of leadership is represented through his mace or gada and his lotus or padma. The mace is like a teacher's ruler, to punish those who do not do what they are supposed to do. While the lotus is rich with nectar and pollen, that attracts bees and butterfly, is for those who do what they are supposed to do.

Ashtalakshmi:

"Om aim hrim srim kleem chamundaye viche" – *Om is a universal sound while aim, hrim and kleem refers to Maha Saraswati, Maha Lakshmi and Maha Kali respectively. Thus, representing all the three feminine forces of the universe combined together.*

"Ashtalakshmi" refers to the eight celestial avatars of Devi Lakshmi.

e. **Adi Lakshmi**: In Sanskrit, Adi means first. Therefore, it refers to the primordial form of Lakshmi, through which she helps a person attain life's foremost aim – freedom from the cycle of death and rebirth. She is thus also known as *"Moksha Pradayani"* or "the one who bestows liberation".

f. **Dhana Lakshmi:** The goddess who brings fortune and prosperity along with her. This form of Lakshmi is always established and worshipped in one's house, workplace, etc. during the festival of Diwali with the hope that the family's business prospers and reaches the ultimate zenith of success.

g. **Dhanya Lakshmi:** The goddess who satisfies one's hunger by providing them food. Dhanya refers to food grains. Food is indeed the foremost requirement for life to sustain. Devi Lakshmi accentuates this veracious statement by her this avatar.

h. **Gaja Lakshmi:** Gaja means elephants. Hence, Lakshmi with elephants. In this aspect, the goddess is depicted seated on a lotus, flanked on both sides by an elephant. According to scriptures, Gaja Lakshmi once helped Lord Indra to regain his lost wealth from the depth of the ocean. This form of goddess is the bestower and protector of grace and royalty.

i. **Santana Lakshmi:** Santana is referred to as child in Sanskrit. To continue the lineage of a family, the birth of a child is very significant. In this avatar, the goddess symbolizes fertility and blesses childless couples.

j. **Veera Lakshmi:** She is also recognized as **Dhairya Lakshmi**. She is a form of goddess Lakshmi that bestows strength and courage during battles and for overcoming difficulties in life. She proves that hope and faith are the most undeviating weapons possessed by a human in order to tackle the adversities brough about by life.

k. **Jaya Lakshmi**: She is also widely known as **Vijaya Lakshmi**, the giver of victory, not only in battles but also for conquering hurdles to achieve success.

l. **Vidya Lakshmi:** The Lakshmi that provides intellect and sagaciousness to a person.

The aforementioned avatars are the eight manifestations of Devi Lakshmi. She presides over these eight sources of wealth. "Wealth" in the context of Ashtalakshmi refers to prosperity, fertility, fortune, health, knowledge, strength, progeny and power.

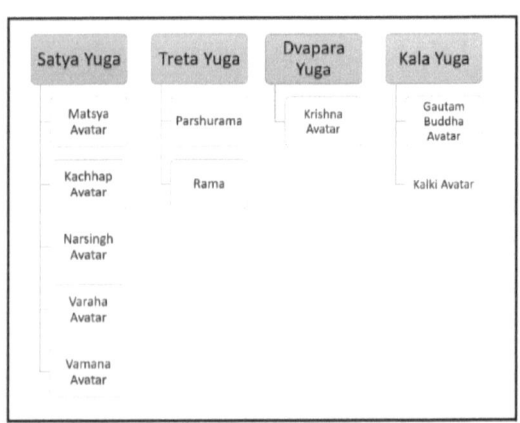

2. The Beginning

Rishi Bhrigu's Curse:

In the beginning of the Satya Yuga, the **asuras** had showed up in front of Mata Kavya's cottage. With her husband, Rishi Bhrigu immersed in his tapasya and son, Shukracharya having embarked on a voyage to the **Pataal Lok** (Land of asuras) due to some unavoidable problems, Mata Kavya was perplexed. She was an amiable lady who ardently believed in what the Vedas and Puranas said. Although she knew that letting the evil asuras in her pure house would be adharma, she was bounded to follow the sacred scriptures that stated *"Atithi Devo Bhava"* – "*Guest is equivalent to God*". The asuras though sinners had showed up on her front door in order to take refuge and she was unwillingly obliged to help them till her son, Shukracharya returned. Having no choice but to follow her beliefs, she let the asuras in.

The asuras took this as a golden opportunity. During the day time, they would seek refuge in Mata Kavya's house and at night attack the devas. Due to her unflinching devotion towards her husband and imperishable purity, Mata Kavya's house was protected by a divine shield that did not allow anyone to enter without her permission. Mata Kavya was compelled to protect the asuras and so she did not invite the devas in.

Indra dev then went running to Lord Narayan and pleaded him to find a solution to this problem. Lord Narayan felt that the only solution to this problem was to either kill Kavya Mata or convince her to throw the asuras out. Devi Lakshmi was bewildered on hearing the fact that her husband said. She warned him not to do any such act for Mata Kavya was her mother. Narayan remained silent as a tear rolled down his cheeks.

He went to Mata Kavya's house and acquainted her with all the problems caused because of her giving shelter to the asuras. However, Mata Kavya was reluctant to escort the asuras out of her house. She instead opted for the other option and requested Narayan to kill her as it would neither break her dharma nor would it destroy the world. Narayan sorrowfully let the *Sudarshan Chakra*; his most powerful weapon slip out of his hand which in turn beheaded Mata Kavya. After the abdication of Mata Kavya, Devi Lakshmi was inconsolable, the devas killed the asuras and Rishi Bhrigu's anger exceeded its bounds. Narayan was well aware about the consequences of his impromptu decision. A frustrated and grief-stricken Rishi Bhrigu held his wife's headless body and outrageously cursed Narayan! He said that just like he had to bear the pain of being separated from his consort, Narayan would be separated from his beloved, Lakshmi in his every human avatar. Since that very day, Narayan is under this painful curse.

Jay and Vijaya:

At the beginning of the process of formation, Lord Brahma created four children who were also called the "Four Kumaras" or the "Chatursana". They were just a product of Brahma's keen desire therefore they were also referred to as the "Manasputras" or "The sons born because of a mere desire". They were named as Sanaka, Sanandana, Sanatana and Sannat Kumar. When they came into existence, they were all embodiments of pure qualities. They did not showcase any signs of negative qualities like vanity, frustration, materialistic desires, lust, attachment, etc. The main motive behind Lord Brahma's creation was that the four kumaras would help complete his duty as the creator by extending their family. However, the Kumaras refused his order to procreate and instead devoted themselves to God and celibacy (Brahmacarya). They requested their father for a boon of remaining perpetually five years old.

Jay and Vijay were the two devoted and determined gatekeepers of Lord Narayan. When the kumaras showed up at Lord Narayan's door, Jay and Vijay prohibited them from entering considering them to be children. They boldly told the Kumaras that Lord Narayan was resting and that they could not visit him then. The Kumaras reluctantly replied that Lord loves his devotees unconditionally and is thus always available for them. However, Jay and Vijay ignored their justification and continued to argue. Narayan wanted to teach his gatekeepers that just like one should not judge a book by its cover, it would be wrong to predict one's greatness and knowledge by their outward appearance or size. So, he knitted a clever plot. He inflicted anger in the Kumaras which in turn led them to curse both Jay and Vijay that they would have to take birth as mortals on the Earth. Immediately, Narayan came out of his abode and Jay and Vijay heartfully requested him to take the curse back. Narayan showed some pity on his loyal gatekeepers and provided them two options. The first one was that they could take seven births as his devotee while the second one was that they could take three births as his enemy and latter be slaid by him. Jay and Vijay wanted to return to Vaikunth at the earliest and resume their prestigious duty of serving Lord Narayan so they opted for the second option. They said that it would be a matter of great pride if they received death by the preserver himself.

Narayan was impressed by his gatekeepers and as decided, Jay and Vijaya took three births in the form of Hiranyaksh and Hiranya Kashyap in Satya Yuga, Kumbhkarana and Raavan in Treta Yuga and Kansa and Shishupal in Dvapara Yuga. They were then killed by Varaha, Narsimha, Rama and Krishna avatar respectively.

3. Matsya Avatar

'Matsya' is a Sanskrit word which means 'fish'. In the Hindu culture, it symbolizes fertility and abundance.

There was a time when all the species in the world were close to extinction. This all started that one fine day when Narayan was immersed in his sleep and Devi Lakshmi decided to tease him. She fetched a vividly colored peacock feather and inserted it inside Narayan's ear in order to tickle him. When her efforts went in vain, she disappointedly threw the feather away. But little did she notice that two particles of Narayan's ear wax have accumulated on the feather's stick. This negligible mistake was the culmination of a long chain of events. Those two wax particles converted into twin demons known as Madhu and Kaitabha. They were twin brother also called the wax demons. With the selfish and irrational motive of conquering the world and gaining supreme power, they relentlessly worshipped Devi Parvati. Unwillingly, Devi Parvati had to grant them a boon. However, she had forbidden them to ask for immortality. After pondering for some time, they let out a vicious laugh and asked the goddess to grant them a wish that they could only be killed by the person whom they choose. Knowing the fact that such a choice would never be made as any person would not want to purposefully invite their death in any kind of circumstances, she had no other choice. Now, Madhu and Kaitabha were almost immortal. They roared like the thunder of the storm that could end the world. They created a seemingly endless havoc in Dev Lok and stole the Vedas and Puranas. Taking this as an encouragement, they mercilessly killed many humans and animals for sadistic pleasure.

Such an atrocious act made Madhu and Kaitabha victims of Narayan's wrath. He challenged both the asuras for war in order to save the world. This battle was ferocious. He battled the sinister brothers without rest for five thousand years. Later, Narayan finally paused to meditate and was acquainted with the boo granted to both the wax monsters. He gave one of his witty smiles and approached Devi Parvati with an unusual request.

He asked her to take one of her most feminine forms and appear in front of the asuras. She readily agreed. As per the instructions given to her, she manifested amidst the asuras. She was enticement personified! The enchanted Asuras had eyes only for the Devi now. They stood gazing at her, aroused past endurance, not knowing what to do. Vishnu took advantage of the situation and asked the asuras to grant the divine lady a boon. In order to impress her, they said that they would grant her whatever she asked for. Devi Parvati momentarily asked whether they could accept death by Narayan for her. Mesmerized by her incomparable beauty they nodded their heads. And Narayan's plan was successful as he took the Sudarshan Chakra and motioned it towards the asuras. Thus, providing relief to millions of people and restoring the scriptures back in their original and righteous places.

However, all this while the damage had already been made. The genocidal war started by Madhu and Kaitabha had wiped out nearly 90% of the Earth's population. In such an alarming situation, Raja Manu (king of all humans) along with his wife Rani Satarupa pleaded to Narayan to find a solution to this devastating war. His land was drained from all kinds of resources and massive unrepairable destruction was caused.

One day, while Raja Manu was taking a bath in the holy river of Ganga, he observed a golden fish with orchid scales all over its body. Its fins were majestic likewise her appearance. Raja Manu was astounded on witnessing such a peculiar creature. He gently placed it on his delicate palms and provided it shelter in a miniature pot filled with water. However, its size increased in a very short period of time and the wooden intricated pot was small for the magnificent fish. So, Raja Manu shifted it to a small lake that he owned. He was thunderstruck on seeing that the pond too turned out to be small for the golden fish. He now had a sneaking suspension that the fish wasn't an ordinary one. He transferred it to an ocean and immediately it disappeared with a yellow light scampering in all the directions. Left behind was an unseen avatar of Lord Vishnu where the upper half of his body was human while the lower half was like that of a fish. Raja Manu bowed in front of the eternal god and thanked him for answering his prayers. Lord Narayan commanded him to create a boat that could give shelter to all the people alive on Earth as they would now have to relocate to a new land. Raja Manu showed pragmatism and instantly fulfilled the task assigned to him.

By the time Lord Narayan had defeated Madhu and Kaitabha, an extravagant and gigantic boat was prepared by Raja Manu. Lord Narayan took his Matsya Avatar. Narayan knew that an ordinary rope would be unable to withstand the immense pressure of the boat. So, he called for Vasuki (the snake wrapped around Mahadev's neck) and requested him to be a part of the solution. Vasuki accepted Narayan's plea and one end of the snake was tied to the horn present on the Matsya's head and the other end was tied to the strongest pillar overboard. With all his might, Narayan dragged the boat and guided it to a new island created by him so that life could sustain.

By taking the Matsya Avatar, Lord Narayan imparted the most crucial knowledge to all beings. He implied that whenever the world's existence will be at stake, the supreme entity shall come to save them. However, for that everyone would have to show their unquestionable faith and trust on the almighty. He made humans realize that by just sitting, hand on hand, the situation would only worsen. One cannot demand something when they do nothing in return. Lord Vishnu says that first one should perform their karma, only then shall god help them out. Had Raja Manu not made the gigantic ship and boarded all beings into it, the Matsya Avatar of Lord Narayan would not have been able to do anything.

Ruupam Sa Jagrhe Maatsyam Caakssusso dadhi-Samplave |

Naavyaa ropya Mahiimayyaam-Apaad-Vaivasvatam Manum | |

He (i.e. the Lord) took the form of a Matsya (Fish) when whole World was affected by deluge. He made Manu ascend a Boat when everything was submerged in water and thus protected them.

4. Kachhap Avatar

Maharishi Durvasa was the son of Devi Anusuya and Rishi Attri. He is known for his short temper. Thus, wherever he went he was received with great reverence from humans and devas alike. If his orders were not executed instantly or his meditation was disrupted by someone, he would immediately curse the guilty! Some scriptures even state that Rishi Durvasa was immortal.

Rishi Durvasa presented an exceptionally beautiful garland made out of the tantalizing flowers of Paarijat (A noteworthy flowering plant only found on the peaks of Kailash.) before Devraj Indra. Lord Indra was captivated by the aroma of the distinctive flower and reached out to grab it. However, Rishi Durvasa resisted his approach and said that he had made it for his Lord Narayan. But he said that if Devraj Indra liked it so much, he could take it. The moment Devraj Indra heard this, his veins were set on fire and he brutally snatched the delicate garland from the Rishi's hand and ferociously said that he is the Rain god and does not accept second handed gifts. He then threw the garland on the neck of his royal elephant, Airavat and said that maybe his pet would accept it. The elephant jerked his head and threw the garland down. Devraj Indra added mockingly that the garland made by Rishi Durvasa wasn't enchanting enough to even please his elephant so how on earth would it make Lord Narayan happy. This was the last straw. Rishi Durvasa's anger knew no bounds he said that Devraj Indra's vanity lies in his prosperity. So, he cursed him that all his wealth would sink deep into the ocean. On hearing this Devraj Indra realized his abysmal mistake and fell on the ground to touch Rishi Durvasa's feet and pleaded for forgiveness. However, the curse was not taken back.

Far away, a droplet rolled down Narayan's blue cheeks as he held Devi Lakshmi's hand. Devi Lakshmi knew that it was time for her to leave Narayan again as after all she was wealth. Whenever a curse related to wealth had befallen upon the world, it was Lakshmi who had to drown in the deep unreachable ends of the ocean till Narayan found out a solution to get his beloved consort back. Narayan begged his wife not to leave him, but she had to respect the curse of her devotee. Momentarily, she vanished into thin air leaving Narayan surrounded by nothing but loneliness.

A few years passed and Narayan told the Gods that the only way to get prosperity and his wife back was by churning the ocean. Mount Mandar- a spur of Mount Meru was torn out to use as a churning stick and was seated at the bottom of the ocean. In order for it to remain stagnant, an exceedingly strong base that could withstand the mountain's immense weight was required. Lord Narayan then took his Kachhap (tortoise) avatar and provided support to the Mountain. Snake Vasuki was called once again and used as a rope. Lord Narayan had somehow managed to convince the asuras to help him in the process of the Samudra Manthan and promised to give them the elixir that would come out from the ocean. The asuras and devas both agreed to this and while the devas held the tail of Vasuki, the asuras held the mouth. Decades passed by and the process continued. One day all of a sudden, a poisonous deadly stinky gas emerged from the ocean. This was called the "Halahal". The only condition for the Manthan to continue was that whatever came out would had to be consumed or brought to some kind of use. Therefore, Mahadev stepped ahead and allowed the Halahal to enter his body. Devi Parvati ran to her husband's rescue and using the power of love stopped the Halahal from spreading throughout Mahadev's body. As a result of this action, all of the poison got accumulated in Mahadev's neck which made it appear blue in color. Since that day, Mahadev was also called "Neelkanth" ;"the one who's neck is blue".

After overcoming this hurdle, finally Devi Lakshmi rose from the depth of the ocean. Her presence was interpreted by all as a divine yellow light cut through the ocean and ignited the sky. The moment Lakshmi opened her eyes, the prosperity, power, extravagancy, love, kindness and purity which were long gone came back. Rishi Durvasa's curse had broken and Narayan got his beloved back. Next came the elixir and immediately the asuras and devas started to vigorously fight for it. At that time, Narayan took an unforgettable avatar.

"The sparkle in her eyes disseminate like the rays of the sun. Her lovely smile adds colors to the flowers. Her dark locks of hair even make darkness as alluring as gold. The speed of her lovely gait determines the speed of the Earth. She is the one who enchants everyone with her physical attributes. Her hands and legs are as soft and a delicate as a feather. Draped in an elegant sari with two anklets tied around either of her legs. With a gold string hanging from her tapered waist. Her nails are carmine red and lips are saccharine. She is none other than Devi Mohini." This feminine avatar of Lord Narayan brought about a smile on the face of the Devas and Devis.

Devi Mohini held everyone mesmerized by her graceful dance moves. She grabbed the elixir and started pouring it in the mouths of Devas and Asuras alternatively. However, the asuras were given normal water and the devas were given the exclusive elixir. As this process went on smoothly, Rahu, a demon began to suspect Mohini's moves. He disguised as a Deva and tip toed into their group. As expected, he had drunk the elixir by deceit. As soon as Mohini had emancipated this, she revealed herself as Lord Narayan and decapitated Rahu with her Sudarshan Chakra. As he had already become immortal after drinking the elixir, he could no longer be killed. But he was cut into two pieces. Since that day his head was called Rahu while his body was named Ketu.

By taking this avatar, Lord Vishnu taught humans that during grim times, it is required to put in one's hundred percent efforts instead of shedding tears or criticizing others for one's loss. Had Lord Narayan repented the loss of his wife or punished Lord Indra for his mistakes, he would have never been able to get back his consort. Sometime it is important to let bygones be bygones and move ahead in life. Another interesting concept accentuated by the God was that at times, one might have to go through extreme scenarios and encounter impossible tasks. But, they should never ever give up and get back what is rightfully theirs. Having both the asuras and devas in the mission of churning the sea seemed to be unattainable but Lord Narayan used his wit and got the task done.

Sura-Asuraannaam-Udadhim Mathnataam Mandaraacalam |

Dadhre Kamattha-Ruupenna Prssttha Ekaadashe Vibhuh ||

When the Suras (Devas) and the Asuras (Demons) were churning the ocean with the Mandarachala mountain, The All-Pervading Lord supported that mountain on his back in the form of a Kamattha (Tortoise), during his second incarnation.

5. Varaha Avatar

Hiranyaksh, a fearless demon stole the planet Earth and hid it underneath water. The reason for the execution of such an atrocious act was that he wanted to weaken the Devas. In order to retain their immortality and celestial powers, the Devas had to perform "Havis" (a Sanskrit word which means "A sacrificial cake"). In this process, they would sacrifice any mortal in order to retain their youth and weapons. With the Earth surrounded by dark waters, the Bhu Devi's (Goddess of Earth, avatar of Lakshmi) life was in peril. The humans were subjected to a brutal death and Bhu Devi's life was slowly ebbing away too! In such a scenario, it would have been impossible to perform the Havis. The devas then reached out to Lord Narayan and relentlessly pleaded for help.

Lord Narayan then took his Varaha or Boar Avatar. He relocated Earth and carried it on his tusks. The moment Hiranyaksh intercepted Narayan's presence, he went out to fight him and commenced one of the greatest battles ever. Lord Narayan had placed the Earth on his thigh and continued to fight. After a few decades,

Hiranyaksh was slain and Lord Narayan had accomplished his task of rescuing the Earth. During the battle, because Narayan had placed Bhu Devi on his thigh, she was blessed with a child. However, the offspring so born was the result of a ferocious war so it was an asura who was called "Narakasura". Later, Lord Narayan had killed him in his 8th avatar as Lord Krishna.

"The avatar of Varaha signifies the restoration of the Earth from a pralaya (deluge) and the formation of a new kalpa (cosmic cycle). Varaha Purana, one of the major eighteen Mahapuranas, describes about the Varaha incarnation of **Lord Vishnu**, and also about the rescue of the Prithvi."

By taking the Varaha avatar, not only did Lord Narayan save the Earth from a deluge and the clutches of an evil monster, the almighty also assured all beings that during the worst time, when all hopes shall drain out from a human being, the Lord will come and fight till the last breath if required to save and protect everyone. As shown, in the Matsya Avatar as well, all he would need in return would be resilience from the side of humans and their undeviating determination and courage. Because, at the end of the day, one has to fight their own battles.

Dvitiiyam Tu Bhavaaya-Asya Rasaatala-Gataam Mahiim |

Uddharissyann-Upaadatta Yajnyeshah Saukaram Vapuh ||

For the welfare of this World, the Lord lifted the Earth which had gone to the Nether World on his tusks; the Lord Who is the Lord of the Yagnas and has the Form of a Boar (Varaha).

6. Narsimha Avatar

Hiranya Kashyap was filled with vengeance on hearing about his brother, Hiranyaksh's merciless death by the Varaha Avatar of Lord Narayan. The only thing that revolved in his mind was to fulfill his brother's long-awaited dream of attaining supreme power. He pleased Lord Brahma by his fervent devotion and was granted a boon. Instantly he asked for a boon of immortality. Lord Brahma had forbidden to give him such a boon as whoever is born is meant to die. Hiranya Kashyap then pondered for some time and said that at least Lord Brahma could allow him to choose his own death. Lord Brahma then answered in the affirmative. Hiranya Kashyap then asked for the following boon:

"May he not be killed by asuras, devas and humans. May he not be killed by either weapons or divine powers. May he not be killed during the day or night. May he not be killed in the sky, land and water. May he not be killed either in the house or outside the house."

Lord Brahma was now perplexed but was compelled to grant him the aforementioned boon. Hiranya Kashyap then laughed demonically and set out conquer the world. His victims were helpless humans. In each and every temple, the idol of God was demolished and his sculptures were established. Ever household had to start their day by worshipping him. It was the rise of an inevitable terror. Amongst this spreading fear and discontentment, Hiranya Kashyap's youngest son, Prahalad keenly worshipped Lord Narayan. He was Vishnu's ardent devotee and feared none when it came to his unconditional love for the preserver. Hiranya Kashyap was annoyed by his son and tried to kill him a few times however all his efforts went in vain and each time Lord Vishnu would save him.

One day he called for his sister, Holika who had been given a divine cloth which if kept on one's head would keep them safe from burning when subjected to fire. Hiranya Kashyap asked his sister to sit in a fireplace with Prahalad on her lap and put the celestial cloth on her head. Hiranya Kashyap would then ignite the fire and Prahalad would be burnt to ashes. Holika readily agreed and as planned, she sat in the fireplace accompanied by Prahalad and her cloth.

However, the moment Hiranya Kashyap introduced the fire, a zephyr blew which in turn led the cloth to fall off from Holika's head to that of Prahalad. This was the exact opposite of what Hiranya Kashyap had anticipated. Holika was reduced to a heap of charcoaled color ashes and Prahalad remained safe. This day is celebrated by all Hindus in the form of Holi. This is a day where one celebrates the victory of goodness over evil.

Hiranya Kashyap's exasperation knew no bounds, he set out to kill his ward. Prahalad then shut his eyelids and reiterated Lord Vishnu's name. Momentarily, growls could be heard everywhere. A peculiar hybrid broke through the pillars of the royal court. It was the Narsimha Avatar of Lord Vishnu. It was a mystical blend of a lion and a human. This exceptional avatar dragged Hiranya Kashyap to the entrance of the palace and engaged him into a fight. He placed the asura on his thigh and teared his chest apart with his exceedingly long nails. It was the time of sunset and blood was oozing out of Hiranya Kashyap. In this way, the boon given by Lord Brahma was not broken yet Hiranya Kashyap died. Post Hiranya Kashyap's death, it was impossible to stop the Narsimha Avatar. His breathtaking roar could be heard in all the four directions. Devi Lakshmi then appeared in front of him and gently held his blood-soaked hands. She repeatedly asked him to maintain his cool. Finally, the Narsimha Avatar came to a halt. Since that day, he is being worshipped with Devi Lakshmi sitting on his left lap while Prahalad seated on the right one.

"A person's heart beats on the left side of his chest. Therefore, his consort always sits on his left. This portrays their immense love and the fact that they are two bodies but one soul."

By taking this avatar, Lord Vishnu proved that sometimes one might feel that a given problem has no solutions. Everyone felt that Hiranya Kashyap was unbeatable. However, if there is a problem, no matter how obscure it may seem, there will always be a solution. Sometimes, a little bit of wit is what is required to get out of it. At all times one should believe that they are not alone and that the supreme power is present within them. All they need to do is appeal to the Vishnu present in their conscience and nobody can harm them. Such was the case of Prahalad. He made it out safely of all deadly situations just because he believed in the almighty and thought about him every time death approached him.

Caturdasham Naarasimham Bibhrad-Daitye[a-I]ndram-Uurjitam |

Dadaara Karajair-Uuraav[au]-Erakaam Katta-Krd-Yathaa | |

The Lord appeared in the form of Narasimha (Man-Lion); and held the king of the Daityas (Hiranyakashipu) who was endowed with great Power on his thighs and he tore him with his Nails, as if his body was a Straw Mat of Erakaa grass made by a Plaiter.

7. Vamana Avatar

Raja Bali, king of asuras performed a sacrificial yagna to gain imperial sovereignty. The devas interpreted that if the yagna would be successfully accomplished then their existence and land, both would be in peril. So, as usual they soke refuge in Vaikunth and asked Narayan for help. However, this time Lord Narayan had planned out everything. He assured the devas to leave the matter entirely on him and he would find an effective solution to it.

The only thing that Raja Bali now needed to complete his yagna which would provide him the epitome of power was a Brahmin. He would perform the concluding rituals and in turn Raja Bali would give him whatever he asked for as *"Dakshina"*.

Far away, a miniature silhouette carrying a straw umbrella appeared. As the figure emerged from the darkness, it became more evident. It was a Brahmin wearing an orangish colored angavastra (Cloth). He was very petit. His entire head was shaved except for a small bunch of strands that stood at the middle of the scalp. He wore sacred threads and beaded jewelry all over his body. It was the Vamana Avatar of Lord Narayan. He said that he would perform the concluding rituals and Raja Bali jovially agreed and accepted his request. Once the yagna was over and it was time to give the Dakshina, the Brahmin asked for land equivalent to his three footsteps. Raja Bali laughed mockingly and agreed. However, Shukracharya warned him that there might be a hidden trick. Raja Bali denied to listen to his guru's advice and granted the Brahmin what he desired for. Immediately, the Vamana Avatar's height increased. He was no longer the short heighted Brahmin, instead he now appeared to be a gigantic giant. In one step he covered the entire earth in other he took over the sky. Raja Bali was astounded he realized that the Brahmin who had performed his rituals was a divine figure. Then the Vamana avatar asked as to where could he keep his third footstep as there was no space. Raja Bali understood his mistake of misunderstanding and not recognizing Lord Narayan's avatar. As an apology, he asked him to keep the third leg on his head which would send him all the way back to Pataal Lok. Lord Narayan smiled and did so.

He made one believe that it is foolish to judge a book by its cover. What may sometimes appear to be harmless and timid may actually be the opposite. Also, it is required to respect people no matter what because one always has to pay for their karma in that same life itself. So, it is irrational to do something that one might regret later on. It is always advisable to think before saying or doing anything because once done, it cannot be reverted and regret is all that will be left in that case. People say it is useless to cry over spilt milk however, the prime attempt should be to refrain the milk from spilling in the first place.

Pan.cadasham Vaamanakam Krtvaa-gaad-Adhvaram Baleh |

Pada-Trayam Yaacamaanah Pratyaaditsus-Tri-Pissttapam ||

The Lord assumed the form of a Vamana (Dwarf Brahmana), and went to the yagya of king Bali. There he asked for three Steps of land, as a result, he took the three worlds (from Bali).

8. Parshuram Avatar

The Puranas record that Parshuram was an aggressive, short-tempered and violent avatar of Lord Vishnu. He was born to a Brahman sage, Jamadagni and Princess Renuka, member of a Kshatriya family. When Jamadagni suspected Renuka of an unchaste thought, he ordered his son, Parshuram to cut off her head. The obedient son did as he was ordered.

Sahastrabahu, the monstrous demon with 1000 hands went to hunt in the forests one day. There he found Jamadagni meditating with his Kamdhenu cow abreast. Sahastrabahu was well aware of the fact that the Kamdhenu cow would fulfill whatever a person demanded for. Out of greed, he approached Jamadagni and asked for his cow as a gift. Jamadagni opened his eyes and politely refused to obey the demon king. Sahastrabahu fumed with anger; he forcefully abducted the Kamdhenu cow. When Parshuram was made aware of this, he killed Sahastrabahu with his powerful axe and returned the cow to its rightful owner. In order to avenge their father's death, the sons of Sahastrabahu killed Jamadagni to induce a moral affect upon Parshuram.

Later, to avenge the brutal death his father had been subjected to by a Kshatriya, he killed all the male Kshatriyas on Earth 21 successive times. Each time, their wives survived and gave birth to the new generations.

He is said to be an immortal; Brahma-Kshatriya as he has played a significant role in both Ramayana and Mahabharata which took place in Treta Yuga and Dvapara Yuga respectively.

By this avatar, Lord Vishnu teaches one the value of acquiring knowledge and learning lifelong. At any point of time in life, one cannot say that they have learned enough. This is because knowledge is a massive ocean and in one human life, it is only possible to get hold of one tiny drop from it after relentless efforts. Another characteristic disposition taught by the Lord is that devotion is the key to everything. Devotion does not necessarily mean praying to God all day long. It may symbolize different things for different people. Constantly concentrating one's thought towards that one source of energy, that one task that provides them the will to live, happiness is called devotion. It is not a onetime act. One is said to be devoted only when they think about their mentor at all times even when they are asleep. One who achieves devotion in its true senses is said to be enlightened and spiritual.

Avataare Ssoddashame Pashyan Brahma-Druho Nrpaan |

Trih-Sapta-Krtvah Kupito Nih-Kssatraam-Akaron-Mahiim ||

On seeing the Kings hostile to the Brahmanas, The Lord (incarnated as Parashurama). He became enraged and twenty-one times he made the Earth free from the Kshatriyas.

9. Ram Avatar

Birth of Lord Rama

The kingdom of Ayodhya was the most prominent and developed city in terms of defense, economy, infrastructure, health and education. For many years, it had been supervised and ruled by the prestigious Raghu Clan. Though a monarchy, all decisions were made with public consent and for mass benefit.

Maharaja Dashrath was a chakravarti emperor and (chakravarti; title given to the conqueror of all the four continents, Pubbavideha, Jambudipa, Aparagoyana and Uttarakuru) the ruler of the Sapt Sindhu. He was married to the princess of Kosala, Princess Kaushalya. With her, he had a daughter named Shanta. Shanta was a blessing for the emperor. She was a brave, congenial, sagacious, rational and genial girl. The king was very impressed with his daughter. However, he was constantly worried about the future of his kingdom after he died. Belonging to a patriarchal society, he needed a rightful heir for his throne. In order to fulfill his wish, he married Princess Kaikeyi and Sumitra.

Years passed by, yet the king could not get a son. So, he approached Maharishi Vashishtha, the raj guru and disclosed his resentment. The maharishi ordered him to organize the Putrakameshti Yagya and please Santana Lakshmi. On doing so, he would be given what he demanded for. But this boon would come at a price. The king would have to abandon his most beloved thing. On hearing this, rumors spread across the palace like fire. Some believed that the king's most precious possession was his treasury while the others thought it to be his throne. However, the answer was far beyond their imagination. King Dashrath's priceless and dearest belonging was none other than his daughter, Shanta. The young princess knew this fact. So, one moonless and starry night, she went to her father, touched his feet and agreed to leave him forever as she could not see tears in his eyes. The king was pleased by his daughter and her iron will. He gave her in adoption to a childless couple, Queen Vershini (Queen Kaushalya's sister) and King Lompad of Angadesh.

A few years later, Angadesh was hit by a drought and millions perished in this famine. It was believed that Rishyashringa (son of Vibhandak Rishi and apsara Urvashi) was a divine figure and could bring rain on whichever land he stepped upon. Vibhandak rishi who was seduced by Urvashi on the insistence of Lord Indra. The couple soon had a son who was named Rishyashringa however as soon as Urvashi's duty was done, she left the rishi and went back to her abode, heaven.

This gave rise to the Rishi's inevitable hate against the entire women race. So, he raised his son in a forest that was isolated from the external world. Rishyashringa had neither witnessed any vices nor had he seen or befriended any human in his entire life except his father.

However, bringing Rishyashringa in Anga was the only way to end the drought in the region. So, princess Shanta was sent to the forest were Rishyashringa was meditating. He was totally amazed to see the princess's magnificent beauty. Shanta was not only successful at mesmerizing the rishi, but could also bring him Anga, thus bringing in rain too. Rishyashringa realized that Shanta was not jot beautiful but also intelligent and strong. So, he decided to marry her and Shanta accepted his offer.

Back in Ayodhya, King Dashrath invited Rishyashringa to organize the much-awaited Yagya. He was awestruck on seeing Shanta. However, it did not take him much time to realize that his daughter was now married. As all the offerings were made, a holy figure emerged from the fire and handed a bowl of heavenly rice. It was latter equally distributed among all the queens. Soon, they gave birth to four sons and the palace had rejuvenated once again. Queen Kaushalya bore Lord Rama; Queen Kaikeyi gave birth to Prince Bharata and Queen Sumitra's twins were named Lakshmana and Shatrughana.

At the end of the day, it was Devi Shanta' s sheer determination that the Raghu Clan was blessed with sons. However, only some scriptures record her self-sacrifice and thereby giving her rarely any credit. Shanta was indeed a divine figure who faced a lot of difficulties in life yet she successfully conquered those. She helped many people and never asked for anything in return.

Note: In scriptures, Lord Rama is also referred to as the following:

- *Raghunandan: Heir of the Raghu Clan*
- *Dashrathnandan: Son of King Dashrath*
- *Kaushalyanandan: Son of Queen Kaushalya*
- *Kamalnayan: The one whose eyes are like that of a lotus*

Birth of Devi Sita

The city of Mithila was ruled by King Janaka and his consort Queen Sunaina. Some puranas often refer to him as 'Raj Rishi' or 'King Sage'. However, the irony in the situation is that both these terms are contradictory. King Janaka, though a king, did not possess any vices. Neither was he captivated by materialistic things nor did he demand power. The soul motive of his life was to search for knowledge and spread the same. Therefore, being a king, his attributes were like a sage. His wife's personality was also unique and discrete from that of others. But years passed by and the couple could not conceive a child.

One year, crops failed in Mithila, millions perished in a famine and this was accompanied by a draught. One of the maharishis advised King Janaka to make a plough out of gold and till the soil thereby impressing Lord Indra, the rain god. A dying man clutches onto the last straw. King Janaka executed the aforementioned instantly. The following day, as the king tilled the cracked soil in the scorching heat, he faced an obstruction. Right in the middle of the field, what appeared to be a huge lump of soil stood as a barrier in his path. The king and his servants relentlessly tried to break the lump however all their efforts vent in vain. King Janaka kept his plough aside and started to dig the ground around the lump. To his amazement, he found a small basket that emitted glorious light in all the four directions. Curiously, he uncovered the basket. What lay inside made him thunderstruck. It was an infant girl, sleeping peacefully. Her face was glowing radiantly. She was surrounded by a godly atmosphere. In no time, an army of grey clouds marched across the sky. Lightning was scampering. This was accompanied by an incessant rain. King Janaka and queen Sunaina clung on to the child who had brought an end to Mithila's sufferings. Streets were filled with children, women and men who merely wanted to feel the rain against their body and see their savior. Janaka and Sunaina decided to adopt this eclectic child thus completing their family. Considering her to be an incarnation of a goddess and on the basis of her existence, she was named 'Sita' which literally meant 'furrow'.

A few years later, Princess Urmila was born to Queen Sunaina. The palace of Mithila had rejuvenated by getting the company of the two lively princesses.

Note: In scriptures, Sita is also referred to as the following:

- *Bhoomija: The one who is born from the Earth*
- *Maithili: Princess of Mithila*
- *Janaki/Vaidehi: Daughter of King Janaka*

Ram and Sita's Marriage:

Years passed by and Ram grew up to be a handsome and fearless prince. He had gained immense knowledge about warfare, ammunitions and supernatural weapons (often referred to as '*astras*') by his tutors Sage Vishwamitra and Sage Vashishtha. He was admired by his subjects for he was obedient, caring and lawful. He believed in extending a peaceful hand towards his enemy at first and if it was rejected, he would wage war. At the end of the day, he was a symbol of 'dharma' and being a descendant of the Raghu clan, he always abided by his promise. Due to his extraordinary principles, he was also recognized as **'Maryada Purshottam'**. Ram had depicted his implicit bravery by defeating the demoness Tadaka and her son, Subahu at a very young age. Later he embarked on his journey towards Mithila accompanied by Lakshman and Sage Vishwamitra. Their solo motive was the seek the blessings of the sacred **Shiv Dhanush** that was given by Lord Parshuram to King Janaka. However, little did the princes of Raghu Clan know that their life was about to change.

On their way, the princes and the sage came across Ahilya's hut. Upon being enquired by the curious princes, the sage narrated a tale from the past.

Ahilya was Maharishi Gautam's wife. She was known for her unwavering devotion towards her husband and purity. One fine day, when Maharishi Gautam went out to seek alms, Devraj Indra disguised himself as Maharishi Gautam and entered Ahilya's hut. Considering Devraj Indra to her husband, Ahilya got intimate with him. Later when Maharishi Gautam returned and he saw Devraj Indra walk away from their house in his original form, the sage got angered. He cursed his wife to turn into a stone statue forever. Later, when he got to know about the entire incident and the fact that his wife was not guilty, he punished Indra for his lowly deeds and said that whenever some prince who is pure at heart and divine would touch Ahilya's feet and forgive her unknown sin, she would return to life.

Ram knew that he was the prince for whom Ahilya had been waiting eagerly for years. He entered the hut and touched her feet thereby reviving her.

*'**Maryada Purshottam'** is a Sanskrit phrase which means "The Perfect Man". Ram was considered as the embodiment of truth and morality. He was always regarded as the ideal son and husband, however above all he was an ideal king. Though born in a patriarchal society, he believed in changing orthodox customs and establishing gender equality. He was a symbol of many good virtues as he was affectionate, kind and generous. Even after thousands of years, he is alive in*

the hearts of millions of individuals. Therefore, he was given the aforementioned title.

According to the Dhanurveda-Samhita(a list that contains 117 weapons), it was believed that the principal architect of all the devas Vishwakarma had crafted two celestial bows and had christened them as <u>'Pinaka'</u> and <u>'Sharanga'</u>. He later gifted these bows to Lord Shiva and Lord Vishnu respectively. Both these powerful and destructive bows were considered to be equivalent to each other. Therefore, some scriptures consider them as twins. Lord Shiva had annihilated many demons using the Pinaka bow and was therefore known as the Pinaki (the one who yields the Pinaka bow). Parshuram had guarded both the aforementioned bows. He had lent the Pinaka bow to King Janaka saying that whichever prince would be successful in lifting it and tying a string to the same would be the most suitable groom for his daughter Sita.

On the other hand, Sita had grown up to be a beautiful and prudential lady. She had developed a deep affection towards nature and would spend most of her time gaining ayurvedic and botanic knowledge. All the citizens of Mithila adored her and would often consider her as an incarnation of Devi Lakshmi herself. She was not a fragile princess like the others, she knew how to defend herself and believed in honesty. King Janaka had announced that he would conduct his daughter's Swayamvar in a short span of time. The guidelines were same as set by Lord Parshuram many years ago. Kings from all over India were invited to join the competition, woe Sita and take her hand in marriage.

When Ram and Sita saw each other for the first time, something inside them knew that their bond was not limited to a life or two. They knew that their relationship was eternal and it was not possible for any individual to anticipate it on their own accord.

During Sita's Swayamvar, many Kshatriyas tested their luck but failed to pick up the Pinaka bow. Finally, it was Ravan's chance. He was one of the most ruthless and shameless kings that the world had ever witnessed. His arrogance had made him consider himself as the most superior and powerful human being alive. He was the king of Lanka (often referred to as the land of gold). He was a keen devotee of Lord Shiva. In fact, he was one of the most knowledgeable kings ever born. However, we know that knowledge can be harmful if not kept under control. This is exactly what happened with Ravan. He could have been one of the most influential rulers in the history of India but his unkempt desire was the reason behind his loss. He too failed to lift lord Shiva's bow. As a result, his ego was hurt, he abused King Janaka and he insulted Sita by saying that she was not a royal blood. He swore to take revenge against Mithila. On seeing Ravan's sudden outburst, the other Kshatriyas took this as an acknowledgement and decided to boycott the Swayamvar. Amidst this chaotic situation, Ram entered the scenario. He joined his hands and showed respect towards the Pinaka bow unlike the other rulers. Then he swiftly brushed his hand across the bow with immense love. He then tightly grasped it and lifted it easily with his one arm. Everyone stood awestruck but

Sita merely smiled. He them broke the bow while trying to tie the string.

Before King Janaka could say anything, Lord Parshuram entered the royal hall with his axe and had sworn to kill the sinner who broke the Pinaka bow. Ram then said that everyone in the hall considered Sita to be a prize of a contest. No one gave value to her humane emotions. Therefore, it was necessary to break the Pinaka so that the arrogance of all the rulers breaks into shatters. Hearing such witty words Lord Parshuram suspected Ram to be an incarnation of Lord Vishnu. However, his speculation turned out to be true when Ram could successfully hold the Sharanga bow that he had given. He asked Ram to oblige him by freeing him from his unconditional anger. On having done so, he blessed the couple and left.

Ram and Sita's wedding was extravagant. People from across India joined to witness this holy matrimony. Amusingly, Lakshman, Bharata and Shatrughana were also wedded to Urmila, Mandvi and Shurtkirti respectively. The Raghu clan was now filled with happiness. They welcomed their daughter-in-law with grandeur. However, their delight was short lived!

Kaikeyi's Demands

Following the legacy of the Raghu clan, King Dasharatha had decided to pass on his throne to Ram for he was the eldest and most worthy successor. On hearing this Kaikeyi fumed with anger and jealousy. She recalled that years ago, she had heroically saved

King Dasharatha's life when he was gravely defeated in a battle. Pleased by his wife's unconditional courageousness, he promised to grant any of her two wishes. Kaikeyi replied that she would ask for her two boons when the right time comes. Kaikeyi knew that that time was knocking on her door. She took refuge in the 'Kop Bhavan'.

Kop Bhavan: Amidst a patriarchal society, the system of polygamy (marrying multiple wives) was quite prevalent, especially among the royals. Therefore, it was quite normal for a wife to feel inferior or dejected. In order to express her vexation and gain her husband's attention, she would take off her ornaments, untie her hair, wear undesirable clothes and thereby enter the Kop Bhavan. This was considered to be a humiliation for the king. On being informed of the same, the king would meet his wife and try to find out an effective solution to her problem.

On the day of Ram's coronation, King Dasharatha went to the Kop Bhavan and asked Kaikeyi the reason behind her exasperation. She then said that she wanted to claim her two boons which were granted to her by him. He replied in the affirmative and asked her to place her demands. Kaikeyi then said that firstly she wanted Bharat, his son, to be declared as the king and secondly, she wanted Ram to go into exile for 14 years. On hearing these wicked desires, King Dasharatha gave his wife an earful and refused to fulfil them. Kaikeyi merely laughed and reiterated a principle of the Raghu clan **_'May you die, but you must always adhere to your promise.'_** On hearing this, King Dasharatha fell on the ground with a thud. Ram entered the Kop Bhavan in search of his father and stood perplexed upon seeing his condition. On knowing his stepmother's demands, he immediately went to his chamber and wore saffron robes. He unfolded the series of events that had happened within the past hour in front of the rest of his family. They were grieve-stricken and forbade Ram to go on exile. However, nothing could refrain him from not abiding by his father's promise. To his astonishment, Sita and Lakshman entered the room wearing clothes alike him. They said that if Ram had the right to perform his duties, then so did, they.

So, Ram, Lakshman and Sita, together went on for the 14-year exile which constituted the major and most integral portion of the great Hindu epic, Ramayana.

Sita's abduction

As the 13 years of exile passed by, Ram, Sita and Lakshman had accustomed themselves to a typical forest life. However, with the passage of time, King Dasharatha had departed from the world. Bharat began his reign over Ayodhya however, he had sworn to return the throne to its rightful owner, Ram, whenever he returned. On the flip side, Kaikeyi repented for her past sins. Urmila was unconscious all these years. The reason being that Lakshman had expressed a selfless, humble and compassionate demand before the Goddess of Sleep. His endless desire to serve his brother and sister-in-law unconditionally throughout their hardships compelled him to work for them day and night. However, his sleep turned out to be a hindrance in his devotional oath. Therefore, he wanted to be deprived of sleep, stress and tiredness for all the 14 years of forest life. The Goddess of Sleep stood perplexed. She then offered a solution to the complex problem. She exclaimed that this could only be implemented if someone would accept Lakshman's need to sleep and be asleep consistently for 14 years. He then said that his wife, Urmila would make such a sacrifice for him. As expected, when the Goddess of Sleep approached Urmila and reiterated her encounter with Lakshman, Urmila replied in the affirmative and promised to open her eyes only when Lakshman returned and agreed to take back his sleep.

Ram, Sita and Lakshman travelled all the way from Prayag to Panchavati. On their journey, they encountered several sages who were ruthlessly tormented by the asuras living in the forests nearby. The two Kshatriya princes obliged the sages by liberating them from the persistent attacks of the beasts. By doing so, they were welcomed with due respect and love. *(Refer to the Map)*

During the last year of their exile, the three royals were residing in Panchavati. One day Ram came across a beautiful demoness named Surpankha. She was none other than Raavan's sister. The moment she was Ram's muscular and lean figure and lotus eyes, she was captivated by him. Instantly she had a lust for acquiring him. In a day or two, she proposed him and Ram rejected it saying that he was already married.

However, nothing could refrain Surpankha from executing her motive. After the failure of her relentless efforts for gaining Ram's love, she decided to murder Sita. As soon as she pounced upon the princess, Lakshman threw his knife at Surpankha which in turn cut her nose. Considering it to be a heartless humiliation she swore to take revenge and took refuge in her brother's palace. Raavan took this as an opportunity to avenge his mortification at the royal court of Mithila during Sita's Swayamvar. He decided to abduct the innocent princess!

After gaining appropriate knowledge about her daily routines, he asked Maricha, a shape transforming demon to turn into a golden deer with silver spots and graze in the vicinity of Ram's ashram. Sita was mesmerized upon seeing the deer. She asked Ram to get the deer for her. In order to fulfil his wife's unkempt desire, he went in search of the mystical creature. A few moments later, Sita heard Ram calling out to her and asking for help. However, it was Maricha mimicking Ram's voice as per Ravan's commands. She anticipated that Ram was in danger and asked Lakshman to go and rescue his brother. Lakshman could neither disregard his sister-in-law's order nor leave her alone in the hut. Therefore, he drew a holy circle around the boundaries of their hut. He titled it as the Lakshman Rekha and forbade to Sita to step out of the circle. He said that no pessimistic power could cross this line. Nevertheless, if they tried to do so, they would be burnt down to ashes. When Lakshman went, Raavan entered the desperate scenario. He tried to enter the hut but he failed to do so. So, he disguised himself as a sage, seeking alms. Sita went into the poorly constructed kitchen and got some fruits for him. Raavan told her to come outside and give her the food. She then told him about all the events that had happened in the past hour and therefore requested him to come inside and take the alms. After arguing for some time, Ravan gave Sita an ultimatum to either step out of the circle orelse she and her entire family would be a victim of his curse. Sita's naiveness compelled her to get out. Instantly, Ravan took his original appearance. Sita had fallen prey to his deceitful looks and as a result he abducted her and took her to Lanka with him in his Pushpak Vimaan (Flying Chariot)!

Ram and Lakshman march towards Lanka

As soon as Ram and Lakshman realized Marich's diabolical plan, they killed him and rushed towards their home. On their way, they found a severely injured Jatayu, fidgeting helplessly on the ground. They were horrified upon seeing that Jatayu's arms were brutally chopped off and blood was incessantly oozing out from it. Jatayu was their ally and had promised to guard them throughout their journey as Dasharatha and Jatayu were friends. When he saw Ravan mercilessly taking Sita with him, he rushed to her rescue. Unfortunately, he could not overpower the powerful Ravan and as a result, he was subjected to such a brutal death. Jatayu then told Ram and Lakshman that it was the Sri Lankan king Ravan who had forcefully taken Sita with him to take his revenge from the princes of Ayodhya. Ram's eyes were filled with anger and vengeance. He vowed to rescue his wife and punish the lawless Ravan as Jatayu took his last breath. Next, they marched towards Kishkindha in search of getting some help from the vanar king, Sugriv.

Vanar: loosely translated as wanderers of the forest. They were human-monkeys who were extremely muscular and extraordinarily strong. They had a huge appetite which was entirely dependent on fruits. Their attributes were like that of humans. However, their physical features were slightly different due to the presence of a tail.

On their way, they met Hanuman, a vanar and friend of Sugriv. He came disguised as a sage. However, Ram immediately recognized him and patted his head. Momentarily, Hanuman took his original appearance and said that he had been given the privilege to live a human life so that he could devote it too Ram. Ram was pleased by his irrevocable devotional spirit and instantly befriended him. Hanuman told him that a feud had arouse between the two brothers of Kishkindha because Sugriv had mistakenly assumed his elder brother, Bali to be dead and thereby began ruling the kingdom on his sister-in-law's request. When Bali returned to Kishkindha, everyone stood awestruck. Before, Sugriv could explain the long chain of events that had occurred, Bali threw him out of the kingdom, held his wife captive and swore to return all these things only if Sugriv would defeat him in arm wrestling. Wining this competition from Bali was impossible because he was way stronger than not only

Sugriv but all humans alive on Earth. Ram promised to help Sugriv if he would lend Ram his vanar army so that he could attack Lanka and rescue his wife. Sugriv agreed to abide by this alliance. Sugriv and Bali looked quite alike. Therefore, Ram told Sugriv to wear a garland while fighting so that it would be more convenient for Ram to shoot Bali. As planned, Ram aimed his arrow at Bali and shot him to death. By doing so he fulfilled his promise.

Lanka at that point of time was a hidden island. No one was aware about its whereabouts. Therefore, all the vanars were told to search for the mysterious and concealed island. After a few months passed by and the expedition turned out to be unfruitful, Hanuman flew overseas and found an extravagant place made of gold. This was Lanka. He found Sita seated in the Ashok Vatika lost in her own world. When Hanuman informed Sita that he was Ram's devotee and came in order to find her, an unceasing river of happiness trickled down her eyes. Hanuman urged Sita to come with him however, to his dismay she readily denied. She said that devils such as Ravan are meant to be punished. She then proclaimed that she would not run away from Ravan's palace like a coward. If she did so, tomorrow he would abduct someone else! Therefore, it was necessary for the benefit of mankind to punish such a monstrous person. Hanuman bowed in front of Sita's greatness. However, before he could depart from Lanka, Ravan's soldiers caught him and presented their intruder in front of their emperor. Ravan commanded them to set Hanuman's tail on fire and let him go to his master. Hilariously, when his tail was ignited, Hanuman flew to every corner of Lanka and set it ablaze. He then went to Ram and enlightened him about Lanka's and Sita's location. Without in any further ado, Ram marched towards the land of gold with his vanar army.

However, when the entire army reached Rameswaram, a barrier stood in between their path. In order to reach Lanka, they had to cross a vast oceanic water body. Nala then emerged as the engineer of the Ram Setu who built an elongated bridge up to 80 miles with the help of floating stones, pumice within only 5 days. Amidst this construction, Vibhishana entered the scenario. He was Ravan's younger brother. Astonishingly, he was against his brother's evil thoughts and practices. He was an ardent devotee of Lord Narayan and always sided with righteousness. Therefore, he wanted to be a part of Ram's army and help liberate Lanka from the clutches of an arrogant emperor. Ram acknowledged Vibhishana's witty decision and allowed him to be on his side during the war.

According to a myth, when the construction of the Ram Setu began, all the stones dropped into the water by Nala began to sink. This was quite obvious as stones had a higher density when compared to that of water. Therefore, Hanuman took a stone and engraved Ram's name onto it with the help of a piece of limestone. To everyone's surprise, when this stone was dropped in the river, it began to float. Therefore, all the vanars followed the same procedure and wrote Ram's name on all the stones thereby establishing the bridge. Since then, people consider Ram's name to be a source of undefined energy.

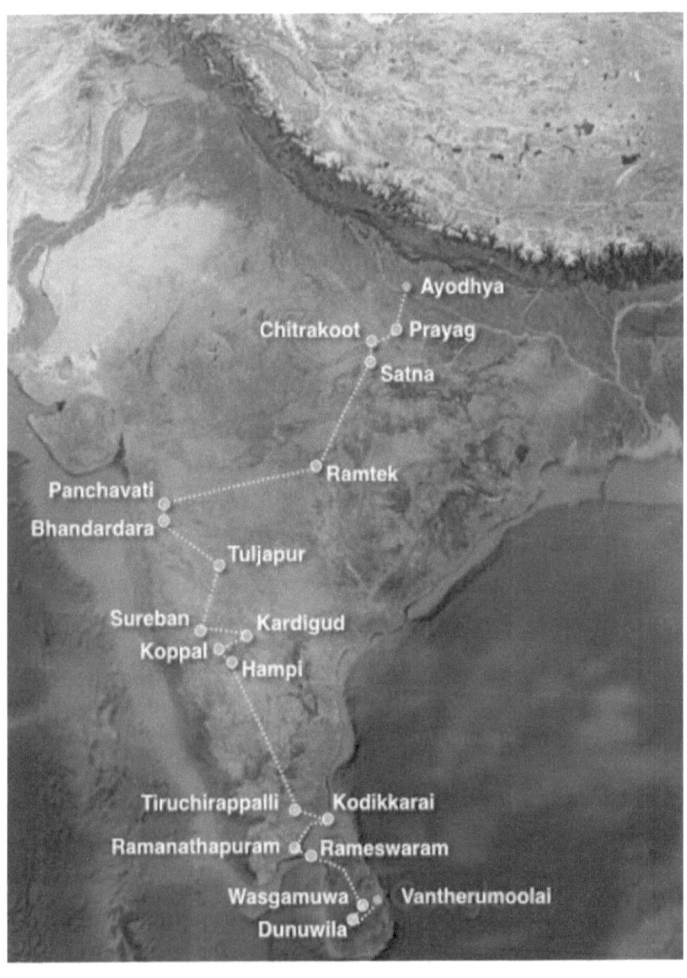

The Epic Battle

The ferocious and unforgettable battle of Ramayana began. Within a few weeks, Ram remarkably assassinated hefty warriors such as Kumbhkarana, Akampana, Dhumraksh and Vajramushti with his celestial weapons. Finally, Meghnath, Ravan's son entered the battle field. He used a divine weapon known as 'Shakti' in order to defeat Lakshman. On seeing his brother's life in peril, Ram's fortitude and resolve shattered into millions of pieces. For a moment, he was ready to withdraw his army and surrender himself. However, an ayurvedic doctor told Ram that only the Sanjeevni herb that was found on the peak of Himalaya could cure Lakshmana and it had to be brought before sunset orelse they could lose their beloved prince forever. Without wasting a second Hanuman went on to accomplish his expedition. On reaching the Himalayas, he saw thousands of mystical herbs and got befuddled as to which was the one that he had to get for his master's brother. So, he chanted a few hymns and his height increased at an alarming rate. Soon he was stronger and taller than the mountain itself! Therefore, he caught hold of the mountain, uprooted it and flew all the way to Lanka with the huge piece of stone in his hand. As a result of his sheer determination, Lakshman was back to normal and took his revenge by beheading Meghnath.

Lastly, when all his assets had perished, Ravan entered the battle field. Ram and Ravan's battle went on for hours. However, very soon Ram realized that Ravan was immortal as every time Ram tried to kill him, within a few seconds he would stand up howling maniacally. Vibhishana then told Ram that there was an elixir in Ravan's navel. If Ram targeted his arrow over there, Ravan would surely die. As instructed, Ram aimed his Brahmastra at Ravan's navel. Brahmastra was the master of all the weapons and Ravan knew that not a single armory would could stop it. As soon as it hit Ravan's navel, blood oozed out from it and he lay dead on the ground. This marked Ram's victory and the triumph of good over evil.

Ram was well aware of the patriarchal society in which they lived; he knew that his citizens would question Sita's purity as she resided in someone else's aboded for approximately a year. Therefore, he told Sita to give an Agni Pariksha.

Agni Pariksha: Literally translated as 'Fire Test'. Since ancient times, people have believed that fire is the purest element in the world. Therefore, when someone had to prove their innocence or purity, they were compelled to step into a wooden pyre that was set on fire. If their body wouldn't perish, people would consider them to be pure and thereby seek forgiveness. On the contradictory, if their mortal body would burn, people would abuse them and their clan. Mostly, women were subjected to such an orthodox and brutal torture. This was later considered to be an evil and meaningless practice and was thereby banned for the benefit of the future generation.

Sita knew that Ram told her to do so because he didn't want his wife to be subjected to any kind of societal shame. Therefore, Sita did as she was told and to everyone's joviality, she came out unharmed.

With this, the 14 years of exile came to an end and Ram retuned to Ayodhya along with Sita and Lakshman and began his reign. Lakshman helped Urmila regain her consciousness. Within a few days, Sita announced the fact that she was pregnant! Everything seemed to be perfect. However, their delight was short-lived.

Ram and Sita's End

One day while addressing his court, a washerman known as Bhadra accused Sita as impure and told Ram to disown her as he wouldn't accept a queen who lived in someone else's palace for a year. Ram tried to resolve his misunderstanding but everything went in vain. Very soon, Bhadra instigated a few other citizens against Sita. They all revolted together. Ram's worst and most fearful nightmare became true. He consulted his elders and tutor by indirectly telling them the complex and tangled situation. All of them told Ram that a king should give his citizens more significance than his personal life and family. Therefore, Ram had no other option but to disown his wife by escorting her to deepest and gloomiest depths of the forest.

As soon as Sita realized that her lord had banished her from his life she fell down with a thud. However, she had to live in order to bring up her unborn kids. She took refuge in Sage Valmiki's ashram. Sage Valmiki knew everything about Sita and decided to preserve their life for eternity. Therefore, as Sita narrated, he wrote down the Ramayana. Within a few months, Sita gave birth to two adorable twins. They were named as Luv and Kush. Sage Valmiki would narrate the Ramayana to them. Meanwhile, Sita concealed her identity from her children because she didn't want her kids to develop a sense of hatred for their father.

11 years passed by; Sita kept dwelling in Ram's memories. When the right time came, Sita informed Luv and Kush about their and her true identity. They confronted Ram by narrating the entire Ramayana and Sita's current situation, thereby revealing their identities in the form of a ballad. Upon seeing Sita, Ram broke into tears and pleaded her to return back to Ayodhya. However, Sita refused to do so and broke into the Earth thus bringing about an end to her life an existence. Ram decided to fulfil his responsibilities as a father and took his kids to Ayodhya.

Years passed by, Ram decided to coronate his kids and renounce the world. Yamraj then told Ram that it was time for him to return to Vaikunth and take his Narayan avatar as Lakshmi and all the gods longed for him. Ram and his brothers then ended his lives by drowning to the deepest depths of the holy river, Ganga.

In order to console the despaired the citizens of Ayodhya, Hanuman tore his chest and showed them a glance of Sita and Ram together. He then said that they were a divine couple who taught the world the essence and power of love. Therefore, they will always be alive in each individual's heart.

Author's Recommendations:

(In order to know a detailed and different aspect of Ramayana refer to these books)

- *Sita (The Warrior of Mithila): Amish*
- *Ram (Scion of Ishvaku): Amish*
- *Raavan (The Enemy of Aryavarta): Amish*
- *Sita (An Illustrated Retelling of Ramayana): Devdutt Patnayak*
- *Ramayana Unraveled (Lesser-Known Facts of Rishi Valmiki's Epic): Ami Ganatra*

A million lessons can be drawn from the Ram Avatar. After all, it is the most well know avatar of Lord Vishnu. He taught the world what it was to live in an ideal society and how responsibilities are more important that anything the world. Performing one's duty (karma) is one's most crucial role. He also taught the world that pain is common to everyone. Be it god or human. If humans did not feel pain, then would they value happiness in the first place? In order to value something it is important to know its price. This exactly what Lord Ram had followed throughout his life and preached as well. Even gods cannot just preach, they have to first do it and show it to the world. Only then are there efforts recognized. One cannot demand fame and immortality in the minds of others by putting in zero efforts. Everyone has to work endlessly for glory and fame. Because the harsh truth is that one can get defamed easily but getting fame is equivalent to a life time's work.

Naradeva-Tvam-Aapannah Sura-Kaarya-Cikiirssayaa |

Samudra-Nigraha-adiini Cakre Viiryaanny-Atah Param ||

He assumed the form of a Naradeva (Divine in the form of a human), willing to assassinate the Suras (Ravana and his army). He suppressed the Ocean which protected Lanka, and performed other deeds of great Prowess henceforth after crossing over to Lanka.

10. Krishna Avatar

Early Life of Krishna

In the Dvapara Yuga, the citizens of Mathura were imprisoned under the rule of a ruthless king, King Kans. To the world he was a brutal emperor, but for his sister, Devaki, he was the most protective and loving brother. When the right time came, Kans married off his sister to the Yadava prince, Vasudev. When the newly-wed couple, went to take Kans' blessing before departing from Mathura, a mystical voice came out of nowhere. It was a prophecy! It declared that Devaki and Vasudev's eighth son would be the reason behind Kans' death. A petrified Kans showed his true colors by imprisoning his dearest sister and his brother-in-law and declaring that he would not only kill their eighth son but all the other children born before him so that he could lead a fearless life. So, years passed by and as soon as Devaki bore a child, the morally corrupt Kans would torment his infant nephews by smashing them against a stone and thereby killing them. Devaki and Vasudev stared helplessly behind the steel barriers tearfully watching their child die.

Finally, during midnight, Devaki gave birth to her eighth son and urged Vasudev to take their child to a safe place where he could be fostered by an ideal couple. However, Vasudev stood perplexed as he couldn't understand how to break open the prison. To their amazement, a melodious tune could be heard and all the soldiers guarding the cell fell asleep and the prison's door opened effortlessly. Instantly, the couple knew that their child was not an ordinary human being. Vasudev kept his son in a bamboo basket and carried him over his head all the way to Gokul. He gave his son to his trustworthy friend Nand and his wife Yashoda who were a childless couple. The couple promised to instill admirable values into their child and allow him to embark on his journey towards Mathura in order to liberate his parents whenever the right time came.

Yashoda and Nand named their son, Krishna. While growing up, Krishna was extensively pampered by his parents and guarded by his elder brother, Balram. (Balram was Nand and his second wife, Rohini's son). During his childhood, he remarkably defeated demons such as Shakastura and Putana. Due to the widespread demonic attacks on Gokul, soon all the villagers shifted to Barsana and later created their own village known as Vrindavan.

A myth goes that Devaki was grief-stricken after her first six children were killed. While she was pregnant with her seventh child, she pleaded with Yog Maya to transfer her embryo to Rohini's womb as she couldn't bear to see another child of hers being brutally killed. Yog Maya accepted her heartfelt request and therefore Rohini bore Devaki's child and Balram was born.

During his youth, Krishna spent a lot of time with the maidens in Barsana. The melodious way in which he played his flute would attract all the girls and they would gracefully dance with him. However, out of all of them, he only fell in love with Radha (an avatar of Devi Lakshmi). She was the daughter of Vishbhan, the sarpanch of the village and his wife, Kirtida.

It was often believed that Krishna enchants everyone with his mystical and notorious behavior. However, Radha on the contrary has always amused Krishna. They encountered endless humiliation, pain of separation and societal mockery in order to teach the world the true essence of love. Even though they were two individual bodies, their soul was one. Their lives were intertwined with each other. By their persistent efforts, they portrayed the fact that love is undefinable and it cannot be beholden within any kind of bond. They never married each other and this did not affect their feelings for each other.

During his early 20s, Krishna had to fulfil one of the main motives behind his birth i.e., to kill Kans and rescue his innocent parents. After tearfully bidding adieu to his foster parents, Krishna and Balram went to Mathura. A ferocious battle was fought between Kans and Krishna and it ended in Krishna's victory. The latter re-crowned his imprisoned maternal grandfather, King Ugrasena as Mathura's king and set free his parents. Krishna and Balram embraced their parents and were thereby subjected to a jovial reunion. However, this was just the beginning!

Establishment of Dwarka

Jarasandh and Kans were allies since decades. After Krishna had assassinated Kans, Jarasandh swore to avenge his friend's ruthless death by killing Krishna. Along with his humongous army, he persistently attacked Mathura. Prince Shishupal and Prince Rukmi also helped Jarasandh in his expedition. In order to save the citizens of Mathura, Krishna built an opulent city that floated on the Gomti river. He titled it as Dwarka because according to him this majestic city was an outcome of his immense love for his people and Radha. Therefore, it was a door that led one to Krishna's heart. He relocated all the residents of his kingdom to this newly established extravagant place. Thereby, he began his reign over the holy city of Dwarka. *(Even after years of research, one still cannot justify as to how Krishna's kingdom floated on water keeping in mind the pressure exerted by it and its citizens onto the Gomti river.)*

Jarasandh's father, King Brihdratha was married to the twin Kashi princesses. He loved both his wives dearly but he was deprived of a son. Therefore, he requested sage Chandakaushika to provide a solution to this problem. The sage gave a fruit to the king and asked him to feed it to any one of his wives and she would be blessed with the kingdom's heir. However, the king could not choose between his wives, so, he divided the fruit into two equal halves and gave it to the queens. A few months later, they gave birth to two halves of a human body. The two lifeless halves appeared to be horror-stricken. As a result, the king ordered his soldiers to throw them in the forest. A demoness named Jara found the two halves and held each piece in one hand. When she brought them closer, the two pieces united and gave rise to a normal living child. Jara did not have the courage to gobble up a child so she presented him in front of the king narrating all the past incidents. The king was elated seeing his son and named him Jarasandh (Joint by Jara).

When Shishupal was born, he had three eyes and four arms. A prophecy proclaimed that his superfluous body parts would disappear when a certain person would take him in his lap and that Shishupal would die at the hands of the same person. Krishna came to visit Shishupal as he was his newly born cousin. The moment he took the infant in his lap, his extra eye and 2 arms shed off, thus indicating that he would be subjected to death by Krishna. Shishupal's mother, Shrutasubha persuaded her nephew, Krishna that he would pardon his cousin, Shishupal for a hundred offences and if he outnumbers the aforementioned number only then he would kill her son.

Amidst this prevalent hatred, Rukmi's sister, Rukmini had fallen in love with Krishna. Hearing about his valor, the fact that he played the flute melodiously and his charming persona, she had solely devoted herself to Krishna without even seeing him. Therefore, she approached her brother and told him that she wanted to get married to Krishna. Rukmi fumed with anger and imprisoned her. He fixed her alliance with Shishupal. Rukmini was devastated. She sent a secretive letter to Krishna expressing her feelings and thereby requesting him to arrive at Vidarbha and take her with him forever. Krishna notoriously smiled upon reading the letter and did as he was told. Rukmi thought that Krishna had abducted his sister, so he waged war against him. However, when he confronted the couple, Rukmini unraveled the truth. Rukmi accused his sister of being deceitful and abused her. Krishna couldn't tolerate a woman being disgraced and therefore punished Rukmi by chopping off all his hair. The latter married Rukmini. In the years to come, Krishna married 7 more princesses namely Satyabhama, Jambavati, Kalindi, Mitravinda, Nagnajiti, Bhadra and Lakshmana. All of them including Rukmini were titled as the *Ashtabharya* or the 8 consorts. They were considered to be Mahalakshmi's 8 celestial avatars with Radha being Mahalakshmi herself.

Narakasura had kidnapped approximately 16,100 unmarried girls. He decided to marry all of them and keep them imprisoned for lifetime. Krishna rescued all of them and executed Narakasura. However, the captivated girls told Krishna that nobody would take their hand in marriage and the society would question their purity. Therefore, Krishna married all those 16,100 girls and saved their lost dignity. At the end of the day, Lord Krishna has 16,108 wives.

Mahabharata

Mahabharata – a timeless battle that changed the principles on which our society was based, turned kinsmen into enemies craving for each other's blood, showcased a woman's wrath after her dignity was attacked, asked for grueling oaths and sacrifices, brought an end to adharma, and purified the Earth. Krishna carved out this entire epic to make the world realize that dharma under any circumstances always outweighs adharma.

The Mahabharata is the battle between two branches of a family – Pandavas and Kauravas. They were the princes of the most influential kingdom in India, Hastinapur. Due to this, even though it was an internal dispute, all the kingdoms of India were involved in this fight due to family ties, trade relations or other purposes. However, we are all aware of the fact that a war doesn't take place in one day. It is the culmination of innumerable factors that is re-ignited by just one act. For the Kuru family, disrobing of the Pandavas' wife, Draupadi was the last straw that threw the entire Kuru family into flames of agony, regret, brutality, and re-establishment of dharma.

The Mahabharata took place in the Kurukshetra and went on for 18 days. It involved nearly 50 lakh soldiers, out of whom no one survived. Apart from the five Pandava princes, the entire Kuru dynasty had gotten engulfed by the flames of adharma. By the end of the war, the Kuru dynasty was left with no successor except one of the Pandavas' Arjun's grandson, Parakshit who was still in his mother's womb during the time of war.

To read about the Mahabharata in detail, you may refer to the following books:

Jaya Mahabharata – Devdutt Patnayak

Mahabharata Unraveled – Ami Ganatra

Bhishma's Oath

The war that changed the pillars on which our society stood firmly began with Shantanu, the king of Hastinapur. He sat perplexed on his throne making the most difficult choice a man could ever be subjected to. A choice between righteousness and lust. A few years back, King Shantanu had married Devi Ganga and she bore him 8 sons. However, due to an impending curse, she drowned all her 7 sons to death and told the horrified king to not demand any explanation cause if he did so she would abandon him forever. The king loved his queen immensely, so he watched all his heirs die in front of his own eyes. Finally, when the 8th son was born, the king could not refrain but asked his queen the reason behind such a heartless act. Devi Ganga narrated an incident from their past life.

Devi Ganga proclaimed that the reason behind her actions was the curse of Sage Vashishtha on the 8 vasus.

In Hinduism, the Vasus are attendant deities of Indra, and later Vishnu. They are eight elemental gods representing aspects of nature. The name Vasu means 'Dweller' or 'Dwelling'. They are eight among the thirty-three gods. Here are the names of the 8 Vasus and their respective meanings.

- Anala meaning "living" or "The Fire"

- Dhara meaning "support" or "The Earth"
- Anila meaning "The Wind"
- Aha meaning "Space"
- Pratyusha meaning "light" or the "Sun"
- Prabhasa meaning "The Sky"
- Soma meaning "The Moon"
- Dhruva meaning "The Stars"

One day, these 8 vasus went on a journey along with their respective wives. On the way, they came across Sage Vashishtha's ashram. Outside his hermitage, they saw the sage's divine cow, Nandini. The wife of one of the vasus wanted to have the cow. Even after being told repeatedly that it was not hers to possess, she remained adamant. Therefore, her husband along with the 7 other vasus took the cow with them. When the sage got to know about this, he cursed the 8 vasus to be born on the earth and undergo immense suffering. The vasus pleaded in front of the sage and asked for forgiveness. Then sage Vashishtha showed mercy on them and said that the curse could not be taken back but it could surely be made less brutal. He said that they would have to be born as humans but they would be subjected to a short life span. After that they could return to Indra's heaven. The vasus then went to Goddess Ganga and told her the entire incident and requested her to give birth to them and drown them thereafter. Ganga agreed to do the same. She then took her human form and fell in love with King Shantanu and bore 8 children out of him she drowned 7. But since King Shantanu had stopped her while she was drowning the 8th child, Ganga told Shantanu that he had broken his promise so as decided, Ganga would abandon him but in return she would take the 8th son with her and train him properly and give him back to King Shantanu when he is in his early 20s so that he could be the fit heir of Hastinapur. While leaving she warned the depressed king that their 8th child would have to live a painful and distorted life.

Years went by and the lonely king waited for his son. After 20 years, Ganga returned with her son who was named Devavrata. Devavrata learnt warrior skills from Parshurama and gained immense knowledge about political and social issues. He was fit to rule the dignified empire of Hastinapur. It is said that no human or animal could defeat Devavrata.

King Shantanu longed for a companion. He found homage in Satyavati, the daughter of the king of the fisherman tribe. Satyavati agreed to marry him but when she learnt about Devavrata, she became insecure. She told Shantanu that since Devavrata would become the future king her progeny would be reduced to the status of slaves. Later, Devavrata's successor would totally disregard her and her future children's existence. The king now had no option but to choose between the kingdom's benefits and Satyavati's insecurities. As expected, the old king could not conclude. On knowing the complex situation in which his father was stuck, Devavrata took 2 grueling oaths.

Firstly, he swore to abandon the throne and secondly, he promised to never marry and have children. Impressed by her son's unwavering devotion towards his father, Goddess Ganga granted him a boon. She said that Devavrata who was there on renamed as Bhishma (the one who sacrificed) would only die when he wanted.

The Jinxed Clan

King Shantanu then married Satyavati and had two sons, Chitrangda and Vichitrvairya. After King Shantanu's death, Chitrangda was supposed to rule Hastinapur, but he lost his life during a battle. Therefore, the queen had no choice but to crown her mentally unstable son, Vichitrvairya as the king.

A few days before Vichitrvairya's coronation, King of Kashi held a Swyamvar for his three daughters Amba, Ambika and Ambalika. All the kings of India were invited except Vichitrvairya. This disheartened the prince, and he asked Bhishma to kidnap the three princesses and present them before him. The elder brother did as he was told. Ambika and Ambalika readily agreed to marry Vichitrvairya however, Amba who was in love with King Shalva abandoned the royal court. On returning to King Shalva's palace, the egoistic king disregarded Amba as he considered her to be someone else's property. A raging Amba burnt herself to ashes but swore to be the reason behind Bhisma's death in her next life.

During Vichitrvairya's coronation, the ill prince died suddenly leaving the court of Hastinapur stunned and without any successor. The widowed princesses Ambika and Ambalika were asked to perform niyoga.

<u>Niyoga is a practice that permitted either the husband or the wife who had no child by their spouse to procreate a child with another man or a woman.</u>

Satyavati called her son Vyasa. Years before meeting King Shantanu, Satyavati came across Sage Parashara. He was smitten by the young maiden's beauty and wanted to get intimate with her. Satyavati was scared that if she denied so, the sage might curse her, so she agreed to it and fulfilled his desires. As a result, Ved Vyasa was born accidentally and given to Sage Parashara to be taken care of.

As instructed by his mother, Ved Vyasa called upon Ambika. Seeing the sage's scattered hairlocks and face covered with ashes, the princess closed her eyes out of fear. Thereby the son born to her was blind and named Dhritrashtra. Since a blind prince could not rule such a great empire, Ambalika was called upon next. On seeing the petrifying appearance of the sage, Ambalika went pale due to fear and the son born to her was yellow and weak and thereby named Pandu. When Satyavati tried to send Ambalika once again to her son, she got scared and sent a maid instead. The son born to her was physically and mentally fit and named Vidura.

Years passed by and the three brothers shared a healthy bond. Caste problems never became a source of tension between the two royal princes and Vidura.

Dhritrashtra was one of the most powerful kings in history. Pandu was knowledgeable as well as brave therefore fit to be the ruler of Hastinapur. Vidura was the most knowledgeable person on earth and was appointed as the minister of Hastinapur. Pandu and Dhritrashtra loved each other immensely but the fact that Pandu was appointed as the crown prince even though Dhritrashtra was the eldest became a source of tension among the two brothers.

When Dhritrashtra reached a marriageable age, Bhishma decided to get him married to Gandhari, the princess of Gandhar. He was aware of her extraordinary beauty and the fact that she had received a boon by Lord Mahadev to give birth to 100 sons and 1 daughter. However, he expected a confrontation from the King of Gandhar as Dhritrashtra was blind. So, he went to the weak kingdom of Gandhar along with his entire army and compelled the king and queen to agree to the alliance. The poor king knew about Bhishma's valor and readily agreed to the same. A night before her marriage the princess got to know that her fiancé was a blind man. On the very same day, Shakuni, Gandhari's elder brother returned from an expedition and got to know about the unjustness towards his beloved sister. On the day of her marriage Gandhari, who feared darkness, took an oath to blindfold herself forever and serve her husband in every way possible. The princess who slept with lamps lit had now thrown herself into darkness forever to save her kingdom and parents' dignity. This angered the sly Shakuni, and he swore to destroy the entire clan of Hastinapur to avenge the torture her sister was subjected to. Therefore, after Gandhari's marriage, Shakuni stayed with his sister in Hastinapur.

Pandu attended a Swyamvar organized by King Kuntibhoj for his daughter Kunti. The princess asked all the princes present a simple question.

'Why did Ram free Ahilya? By doing so did he not forgive someone who was guilty?'

Many princes replied that Ram was know for his forgiving nature and so he freed Ahilya. However, Kunti was not impressed by these answers. Finally, Pandu stood up and reiterated the entire tale of Maharishi Gautam, Ahilya, and Devraj Indra. He said Ahilya was not guilty of the sin everyone thought she had committed. Devraj Indra had deceived her by his looks thereby compelling her to involve herself in and illicit affair. Gautam Rishi was unaware of this fact when he cursed his wife. Later when he realized his mistake, it was too late. Ram knew that Ahilya's punishment was nothing but penance because she had lost her purity at the end of the day. Therefore, Ram knew that Ahilya had suffered enough, and it was high time that she was forgiven for something she never did purposefully. Pandu then explained the difference between a sin and a punishment. He said that sins are permanent and therefore they can be forgiven not resolved but punishments are temporary and get over with time. Ram did not forgive Ahilya he knew that her punishment was over. Kunti was enchanted listening to Pandu's answer and instantly agreed to marry him.

A few months after their marriage, Pandu married Princess Madri, daughter of King Bhagavana of Madra kingdom. Later he was coronated as the king of Hastinapur. However, a tragedy changed everything.

One day while out hunting, Pandu came across two deer and shot one of them dead. Later he realized that the deer were the sage Kindama and his wife who were disguised in the form of deer to spend some time alone. Pandu had mistakenly shot the sage's wife. The remorseful sage cursed Pandu to die the very moment he tried to get intimate with either one of his wives. Petrified and guilt stricken by his actions Pandu renounced his throne and decided to give up all materialistic desires. He then made a small hut in the middle of a forest and lived there with his wives. Meanwhile, back in Hastinapur, Dhritrashtra was crowned as the king.

Birth of Pandavas and Kauravas

A few months passed by and Pandu longed for a child. Kunti then told her husband a boon that she had gotten years ago. She said that one day she came across Rishi Durvasa. She attended the sage and provided him with food. Impressed by the little princess and her values, he gave her a boon that she could summon any god and ask for a child from him. Pandu was delighted upon hearing this.

Firstly, they summoned Dharmraj, the god of dharma and Kunti bore a son named Yudhistir. Next, they called upon Vayu, the god of power and fostered a child named Bhima. Finally, they asked Devraj Indra, the king of all gods for a son and christened him as Arjuna. On the other hand, Madri also longed for children. Therefore, Kunti shared the mantra with her, and Madri summoned the Ashwini kumaras and gave birth to two boys namely Nakul and Sahadev. The five sons of Pandu were called the Pandavas. The five brothers grew up with each other. They all could die to protect their sibling. They were like the five fingers of a hand that together formed a fist. Pandu himself trained his five sons.

Yudhistir was known for his righteousness and the fact that he never lied and the weapon in which he mastered was the spear. Next in line was Bhima, he had an immensely large and unsatiating appetite, but he was the most powerful being on Earth and mastered in the mace fight. Arjuna was knowledgeable, he knew when to show rage and when to be calm/composed. He was one of the best archers that history had ever seen. Nakul had immense idea about herbal remedies and treatment and aced in the sword fight. Last but not the least, Sahadev could see the future, but he could never disclose it to anybody, and he was known for mastering the axes.

Back in Hastinapur, Gandhari was also pregnant. She had gotten a boon that she would give birth to 100 sons and 1 daughter. However, she remained pregnant for 2 years. This angered Dhritrashtra and to torment his wife, he got intimate with Gandhari's maid, Sughada and she gave birth to a son named Yuyutsu. Finally, when Gandhari got into labor, she bore a ball of flesh. Ved Vyas was then called upon and asked what had to be done with the flesh. Ved Vyas broke it into 101 pieces and kept them in earthen pots. He said that when the right time came, all these pieces would grow into infants. Gandhari and Dhritrashtra waited eagerly for their children. The first child was named Duryodhana, the second one was called Dushasana and so on. Gandhari's daughter was called Dushala. They were all collectively called the Kauravas.

Tradegy Befalls Upon the Pandavas

Years passed by. When the Pandavas were enjoying their teenage life, a tragedy ruined everything. One fine day, Pandu was staring at his beautiful wife, Madri plucking flowers in the garden. He could not refrain himself from getting intimate with her. As a result, the curse took effect resulting in Pandu's immediate death. Madri was guilt ridden seeing her husband's corpse and died too, thereby leaving the responsibility of all the five Pandavas to Kunti. As the news of Pandu and Madri's death reached Hastinapur, Satyavati along with Bhishma went to perform his last rites only to bring Kunti and the Pandavas back to Hastinapur. Satyavati blamed herself for her husband's, sons', and grandson's death. She realized how selfish she had been all these years. So, to repent for her sins she decided to renounce all materialistic desires, leave the palace, and become a sage.

Back in Hastinapur, Shakuni had implanted seeds of hatred in the minds of all the Kauravas against the

Pandavas. As a result, when the five grief struck princes arrived at Hastinapur, they were mistreated by Duryodhana and his brothers. But the Pandavas retained their calm. They stuck to their ideals and principles throughout. Duryodhana's sole motive was to become the next emperor of Hastinapur but upon Yudhistir's arrival, that ambition would be broken into pieces.

The enmity between the Pandavas and Kauravas reached its peak when Duryodhana tried to poison Bhima and throw him into the river. Though Bhima did return to life, his mind was now filled with revenge. He told his mother and brothers the misdeed of the Kauravas and wanted to seek justice. Upon approaching the king, Dhritrashtra and narrating him the entire series of events, the Pandavas and Kunti did not take time to realize that the emperor was reluctant to punish his own son. Bhishma then took the matter in his hands. He decided to forgive Duryodhana for the last time and send all the princes of the Kuru family for training under the renowned sage Dhronacharya.

The Kuru Princes Get Trained

Dhronacharya performed his duty of training the Kuru princes with diligence. He helped all the princes realize their true potential, gain knowledge about warfare and master the weapons they liked. Among all his disciples, the sage had great expectations from Arjun. This all started with that one incident.

On their very first day, Dhronacharya asked all the princes to gather around a tree. On observing their surroundings, the perplexed princes found a wooden bird sitting on the tallest branch of the tree. Dhronacharya called each prince one by one. He asked them to aim at the bird's eye with the help of an arrow and bow. Before, giving them permission to release the arrow, the old sage asked everyone the same question, 'What did they see?' A few replied, the bird, while others said the tree and so on. Unimpressed by their answers, he would ask each prince to keep the weapon aside and go back. Then came Arjun. On being asked the same question, Arjun replied that he could only see the bird's eye. A smile spread across the sage's wrinkled face, and he commanded Arjun to shoot the arrow which went right through the bird's eye. That day Dhronacharya knew that Arjun would one day make history.

One day Dhronacharya saw a tribal boy, Eklavya. He was camouflaging behind a bush and observing the sage teach Arjun archery. Dhronacharya called the boy out and asked him to explain his actions. Eklavya then asked them to follow him. He guided Dhronacharya and Arjun to his cave. There they were astonished to find Dhronacharya's idol, loads of arrows, a bow, etc. Eklavya then said that he belonged to a tribe were learning archery was prohibited. However, it was his dream to become the world's best archer. So, one day while walking in the forest, he came across the sage's hut and saw him teach Arjun. Seeing the sage's commendable knowledge, he decided to pick up archery skills from him. Dhronacharya could not believe his ears, he asked Eklavya to portray his talent and he did. The sage was astonished. Just by listening and seeing someone else practice, Eklavya learnt archery such was his dedication. Dhronacharya, however, was determined to make Arjun the most renowned and unbeatable archer in the world. With Eklavya around, that was not possible. So, Dhronacharya decided to use treachery. He told Eklavya that since he learnt this art from him, he would have to pay him back. The poor lad agreed. Dhronacharya asked for his right thumb and the boy did so. That day, Dhronacharya knew that he had committed a sin but he had no option.

12 years passed by; all the princes had completed their training. On returning to Hastinapur, the princes were welcomed by their family members. They exhibited their talents in front of the royal family. They were indeed smitten. The king then asked Dhronacharya to ask whatever he wanted as his fees. Dhronacharya wanted revenge. He asked the Kuru princes to attack the king of Panchal, Drupad and avenge his humiliation. Drupad, the crown prince of Panchala and Dhronacharya studied together. They were best friends at one point of time. Drupad had promised to help his friend whenever he was in need of the same but materialistic desires change everything. Drupad soon became the King of Panchala. One day, a poverty stricken Dhronacharya, went to his old friend and asked for some money. The miser king refused to recognize his old mate, embarrassed him and abused

him too. Now, it was payback time! The Kuru princes defeated Drupad and gave away half of his kingdom to Dhronacharya. Dhronacharya's son, Ashwathama was crowned the king of that half.

Drupada had a daughter Shikhandini who was the reincarnation of Amba, the princess of Kashi, the reason behind her birth was the death of Bhishma. Drupad could not bear defeat. He organised a holy prayer and bore a son named Dhrishtadyum to kill Dhronacharya. However, as per the prayer, the king would have to accept a daughter along with a son. Drupada already had one daughter and did not want to father any other girl child. But God had something else planned out. From the burning pyre, emerged the most beautiful maiden in the world, Draupadi.

Back in Hastinapur, the princes came across Karna. He claimed to be an archer who could compete with Arjun. During the face-off between them, as Arjun's arrow was about to kill Karna, a golden shield and pair of earrings emerged from his body. Kunti, who was witnessing everything from above stood awestruck.

Karna was the adopted son of a charioteer, Adhiratha and his wife, Radha. Being a shudra, he was considered ineligible to gain knowledge regarding warfare. Since childhood, the young lad loved to do archery. On learning that all the Kuru princes had gone to Dhronacharya's hermitage to receive training, he too followed them and requested the sage to teach him archery but that was against the principles of the society, so Karna was asked to go back from where he came. However, this could not waver Karna's determination to become the best archer in the world. He then decided to go to Parshuram in the hope of accomplishing his dream. He later got to know that the sage only taught Brahmans. So, for the next 10 years of his life, Karna decided to disguise himself as a Brahman. Years passed by Karna turned out to be an excellent archer. One day, Parshuram was sleeping, and Karna sat beside his mentor fanning him with a piece of cloth. Out of nowhere a scorpion came near the sage's feet. Karna caught hold of it and held onto the scorpion to make sure that his teacher's sleep was not hindered. The young boy's hand bled profusely but he bore all the pain for an hour or so. Finally, when the sage woke up and got to know about the entire incident, he was aghast and angrily claimed that Karna was not Brahman. This is because Brahmans barely have any resilience, they cannot endure pain for a long time. Karna then disclosed his identity. Parshuram felt deceived. He cursed Karna that the day he would immensely need Parshuram's teachings, and the knowledge imparted by him, Karna would forget everything for a short period of time. Karna thereby returned to Hastinapur and fell in love with a young maiden named Vrushali and they both got married.

This brings us back to Arjun and Karna's face off. Guru Kripacharya, a council member of the Kuru kingdom intervened during the fight. He said that this battle could not take place as Karna was a shudra and thereby he could not stand opposite to a kshatriya prince. Karna was humiliated. Duryodhana then stepped up and decided to crown Karna as the king of Anga thereby making him eligible enough to fight Arjuna. Since that day, Karna was an obliged friend of Duryodhana, and he swore to protect him and be always at his side. Duryodhana had now found an ally who could defeat Arjun.

The Deathly Ploy

Soon after the princes returned to Hastinapur, Bhishma decided to crown Yudhistir as the king of Hastinapur. Dhritrashtra was not very fond of the decision made but he could not defy his grandsire after all. However, Shakuni and Duryodhana had something else in mind. They decided to terminate the Pandavas once and for all, thereby making Duryodhana the crown prince. Shakuni knitted one of the most cunning and deadliest ploys that history would ever witness. In a place called Varnavrat, Shakuni and his nephews asked Purochan, their messenger, to construct a palace made of combustible substances such as wax, cotton, cloth, etc. The palace was wickedly crafted in such a way that if one corner caught fire, the entire palace would be burnt into ruins within just 6 hours. No lamps were ever lit in that palace, the sole source of light was the moon. Vidura got to know about Shakuni's hideous act. He then asked his workmen to build a secret tunnel in the inflammable palace that would lead the princes and their mother to the nearest riverbank. He then arranged a fully facilitated boat for them. Later, Shakuni and Duryodhana gifted that palace to the Pandavas and their mother Kunti and asked them to go and live there for a few weeks. At first the Pandavas were suspicious and refused to go to such an uncanny palace, but Kunti insisted her sons to accept the gift given by their brothers and uncle. A few moments before their departure, Vidura called the Pandavas and told them about the entire conspiracy and the secret getaway. At first the Pandavas were aghast and demanded justice, but they knew that they could not seek the aforementioned in Hastinapur. So, they decided to fake their death. They all went to Varnavrat and one night while Purochan was fast asleep, the Pandavas set the palace on fire and got away with the help of the tunnel with their mother. Purochan became a victim of his own ploy. On reaching the riverbank, the Pandavas found the wooden boat and asked the sailor to take them to the nearest forest. The Pandavas along with their mother decided to live a life of peace and contentment in the forest as they did before Pandu's death. Back in Hastinapur, everyone except Vidura assumed the Pandavas to be dead.

The Pandavas Get Married

and found a weeping woman. She said that this part of the force was a victim of dark magic. She then proclaimed that she had been trapped there for nearly a week now. The Pandavas was overcome by curiosity, they wanted to find out what was wrong with the forest. They took the scared maiden along with them. Within a few hours, they realized that they had returned to the place where they started. This horrified them but they continued to walk. After an hour or so, they came across a cave. After a while they realized that they had been trapped. All passages for entry and exit had been closed. The strange girl then called out to someone in her local language. From the darkness emerged an extraordinarily tall and muscular man. He was Hidimba, a demon. The girl was none other than his sister, Hidimbi. They both had been hungry since days and awaited someone's arrival. When they spotted the Pandavas from a distance, they carefully knitted the entire plan. A short-tempered Bheem fought with Hidimb and killed him eventually. By now, Hidimbi had fallen in love with Bheem. She asked for forgiveness and begged Bheem to marry her and thereby become the ruler of that region of the forest. Bheem accepted the grief-stricken lady's request. He married her and bore a child named Ghatotkach with her. When the boy was a year old, Bheem left her and Hidimbi in the forest and moved on. Hidimbi and Ghatotkach were not allowed to come to Hastinapur after all they were demons and that would bring upon shame and dishonor to the prestigious clan of the Kuru.

Months passed by Pandavas got to know about a Swyamvar being organized by Drupad, the king of Panchala for his extravagantly beautiful daughter, Draupadi. The competition was that of archery. The reason being that young maiden wanted a husband who was pious and heavenly as the great lord Shiva himself. The entire world knows what a splendid archer the god is, so Draupadi requested her father to keep archery as the field of forte in her Swyamvar. Princes from all over India were invited. Arjun too wanted to take part in the Swyamvar. A long time ago, while he was out fetching wood, he came across Draupadi's chariot. The moment they saw each other, they both had fallen in love. So, Arjun along with his brothers went to the Swyamvar as Brahmins. Warriors such as Shishupal, Jarasandh, Duryodhana, Karna, etc., were all there. Upon seeing Duryodhana and Shakuni the Pandavas were enraged but they somehow controlled their anger. The rules of the competition were quite clear. Quite far up in the sky was the image of a golden fish whose reflection could be spotted on a magnifying glass placed on the ground. The contestant had to lift a bow which was very heavy as it was that of Lord Shiva's and aim it as the fish's eye by looking into the glass. Each opponent came up but failed to even lift the bow. Then came Karna, the moment he held the bow, Draupadi intervened by saying that she would not marry the son of a charioteer. A humiliated Karna abandoned the court immediately. After all the princes failed in completing the task and the Swyamvar was open to one and all present. Arjun stepped out and successfully completed the challenge. Draupadi thereby got married to him. However, Arjun could not start a new phase of his life with a lie. After leaving the court, Arjun told the entire truth to Draupadi, and she showed no reaction. She said that she had known his truth all along. This is because a friend of hers had indirectly told her about the entire incident. Arjun asked Draupadi who this person was. With a smirk on her face, Draupadi said Krishna who had been there throughout the Swyamvar as a spectator.

On reaching their home, Arjun enthusiastically went to his mother to tell her about Draupadi. Kunti was worshipping in front of her clay idol. Arjun's eagerness knew no bounds, He interrupted her mother in between and said that he had won a priceless possession. Kunti, who was immersed in her prayers told Arjun to share whatever he had gotten among his five brothers. On hearing this all the Pandavas along with Draupadi stood aghast. Finally, when Kunti rose and realized her mistake, she was overcome by a sense of guilt. She asked for forgiveness, but words once said cannot be taken back. For the Pandavas, every word told by their mother was as important as a command. They could not defy it. So, this left the Pandavas with two options. The first was that Arjun and Draupadi would live a happily married life while the other 4 Pandavas would have to renounce the world and live on the top of a mountains as sages. The second one was that Draupadi would marry all the five Pandavas. Kunti was reluctant to go by the first and Draupadi disagreed to marry 5 men! Thus, to solve such a dilemma, Krishna came into the scene. Krishna asked Draupadi to marry all the five Pandavas. On hearing this, the already traumatized princess was horrified. She said that in a patriarchal society where women were constantly questioned, asked to maintain their dignity, and never had a say of their own, if she would marry 5 men, the world would consider her impure and she would always be subjected to disgrace.

Krishna then politely calmed the vehement princess and said that the Pandavas are the result of Sage Durvasa's boon. They were born to accomplish a task that would change the world and bring back dharma. Their strength lies in each other. If they were to be separated it would destroy them mentally and physically. Krishna then assured Draupadi that nobody in the world could ever question her purity as she was born from the most holy element of the earth, fire. Whoever tried to harm her dignity would be burnt instantly. Draupadi agreed to marry the Pandavas. However, all 6 of them took a few vows during their marriage. Firstly, Draupadi would spend one year with each Pandava and at that time the other four princes would not enter her chamber or touch her and if they did, they would be subjected to one year of exile. Secondly, at the end of each year, Draupadi would perform a rigorous penance to purify herself and all her five husbands would sit with her throughout the process. Lastly, if the Pandavas ever marry another woman, she would not be allowed to enter the kingdom. With this, the Pandavas returned to Hastinapur to seek blessings from their elders and demand for justice.

The Making of Indraprastha

Back in Hastinapur, the Pandavas asked Dhritrashtra to equally divide the palace, wealth and all the estates under the control of the Kuru Dynasty among the Pandavas and Kauravas. However, an instigated Duryodhana disagreed to give even an inch of his land to the Pandavas. However, after hours of conversation with his wicked uncle, Shakuni, he finally agreed to give the region of Khandavaprastha to the Pandavas. However, Khandavaprastha was a deserted region that was cursed. There was no source of food, water, or shelter there. But the Pandavas accepted their fate as they were not in the position to revolt Duryodhana or Dhritrashtra's decision. On reaching the isolated Khandavaprastha, the Pandavas realized that the only way of building an empire in that area was to burn the rusting forest and start everything anew. Only Agni, the fire lord himself, could perform that task. However, every time he tried doing so, Lord Indra would make it rain thereby putting all the Pandavas and Agni's efforts in vain. However, this time the Pandavas fought against Lord Indra. Even when Lord Indra attacked Arjun with his lightning bolt, the fearless prince stood his claim. Finally, Lord Indra surrendered in front of the unwavering courage of Arjun and his brothers, and the entire forest was burnt to ruins thus allowing the Pandavas to build their palace, their home. Agni was so impressed by Arjun's resilience that he gifted him the Gandharva bow. It was one of the most powerful bows in the world that never missed its target. It was designed by Lord Brahma himself. Later, Mayadev, the lord of delusions, helped the Pandavas create the most extravagant palace on Earth. It was filled with mystical creatures, invisible pathways, hell-bent beauty, etc. Khandavaprastha was now filled with all kinds of luxuries a kingdom could ever have. Arjun was thankful to Lord Indra for allowing them to fulfil their task. So, he decided to rename Khandavaprastha as Indraprastha. Now, the Pandavas wanted to perform a Rajsuya Yagya before beginning their reign over their new kingdom. They invited all the kings of the Arya region. For the Yagya to be completed successfully, 100 cows were required. The night the cows were being transported to Indraprastha, Takshak, the king of snakes stole the cows. The fire initiated by the Pandavas in Khandavaprastha killed Takshak's army of venomous snakes. He swore to take revenge thereby kidnapping all the cows. When Arjun got to know this, without thinking twice, he barged into Draupadi's room though she was meant to spend that year with Yudhistir. He grabbed his Gandhav bow and defeated Takshak and got all the cows released. However, back in Indraprastha, all the four princes and Draupadi could think about was about Arjun breaking his marriage vow. He entered Draupadi's room when he was not supposed to so as per the punishment, he had to spend 1 year in exile. Arjun knew the consequences of his action. He went back to his brothers to seek their blessings and went to pay for his deeds. Yudhistir decided not to perform the Yagya in Arjun's absence. 6 months later, Arjun came across Subhadra, Krishna's sister. They both fell in love with each other however, Subhadra's alliance was fixed with Duryodhana. On the day of her marriage, she begged Arjun to take her with him. However, by doing so, Arjun would start a war with the Yadavas, and he could not afford that. So, Krishna asked Subhadra to abduct Arjuna. In that case, Subhadra would be the one held guilty, and the

Yadavas would not wage a war against their own sister. Subhadra smirked and understood her brother's ploy she held Arjun's hand and kidnapped him! Later they both got married. The day Arjun's exile ended, all that he could think of was Draupadi's distress on knowing that Arjun got remarried. So, Krishna whispered a few words in Subhadra's ears and gave her his flute. He then asked Arjun to embark towards Indraprastha. As expected, Draupadi was outrageous seeing Subhadra and was reluctant to allow her to enter the kingdom. She said that as per the marriage vows taken by Arjun, Subhadra was forbidden to enter Indraprastha. Subhadra then gave Draupadi Krishna's flute and told her whatever Krishna had said. A furious Draupadi quit her anger and welcomed Subhadra. Arjun was astounded but was happy that things got sorted out. Everything was back to normal, so the Pandavas decided to perform the much-awaited Yagya. But this was just the beginning of a dreadful future.

Duryodhana's Insult

All the kings of the Aryan region were invited to Rajsuya Yagya organized by the Pandavas including Duryodhana and Shakuni. The moment he entered Indraprastha, Duryodhana's eyes popped out seeing the extravagance he was surrounded by. He could not come to terms with the fact that the Pandavas had built a heaven out of the hell they got. Jealousy and vanity took the best of him when he saw Yudhistir preparing himself to ascend the crown of Indraprastha. He was hell bound to stop the coronation of Yudhistir. He examined every nook and corner of the court room. Momentarily, his eyes laid upon King Shishupal, ruler of the Chedi kingdom and he smirked. As he hesitantly approached, the king a cunning plot took birth in his mind. The whole Arya region was aware that King Shishupal and Krishna were not on good terms especially after Krishna eloped with Rukmini who was supposed to marry Shishupal. Duryodhana decided to use Krishna's and Shishupal's enmity to stop Yudhistir's coronation. He instigated Shishupal to humiliate Krishna who was standing near the Pandavas. The Pandavas would not tolerate Krishna's insults and would draw out their weapons against Shishupal thereby creating a state of war. This would result in the postponement of Yudhistir's coronation, giving Duryodhana time to think as to how he could trap the Pandavas into giving up their newly built palace. A short-tempered Shishupal fell victim to Duryodhana's selfish ploy and stood from his chair. He started mocking Krishna by claiming he had 16,108 wives. Then he questioned Radha's character. Radha, the love of Krishna's life. He called Krishna treacherous and a coward. The moment the Pandavas asked him to stop, he unfurled his anger at them and termed Draupadi as a characterless woman for she had 5 husbands. He called the Pandavas illegitimate sons of Pandu. Finally, he insulted Pandu by calling him a docile and meek king. But throughout these series of humiliations, an agitated Shishupal forgot that as per the boon granted to him, only 100 of his mistakes would be pardoned by Krishna. And Krishna waited. As soon as, Shishupal tried to kill Krishna with his arrow, he had made 100 mistakes! Before he could realize this, Krishna summoned his Sudarshan Chakra and beheaded Shishupal. Since then, it is said that outrageous words can be the reason behind one's befall. Duryodhana's plan went in vain as Yudhistir descended on the throne along with Draupadi. The ceremony was over and Duryodhana was about to leave the palace. On his way out, he tripped on a carpet and fell into a pool. Draupadi and a few of her maids witnessed this. One of the maids said that a blindman's son is also blind. On hearing this, a furious Duryodhana turned around with a jerk to see who made the comment. His eyes fell on Draupadi who was smiling. He assumed Draupadi to be the one who insulted him and swore to take revenge. He decided to dishonor her in the most tragic way possible that the world would remember.

The Disrobing of Draupadi

Years passed by. Draupadi bore 5 sons. One from each of the Pandavas. Subhadra was also pregnant with Arjun's child. However, one fateful day, an invitation to a game of dice sent by their brother, Duryodhana changed everything. Little did the Pandavas know that accepting it would be the biggest mistake of their life. Meanwhile, back in Hastinapur, Duryodhana and Shakuni made all the arrangements for the game. Well, there was a reason behind all of this. A very dark one. The dice that were being used to play the board game were Shakuni's and pretty much magical. Whatever number Shakuni would think of would appear on the dice. A legend says that the dices were made using Shakuni's dead father's bones. Shakuni's father loved him after all he was his only son. He pampered his lad endlessly and promised to always fulfil his wishes and make his dreams come true. As a result, even after his death, his bones continued to work as per Shakuni's demands. As the Pandavas and Draupadi came to Hastinapur, the five princes were escorted to the royal court where all the hundred Kauravas, ministers, Bhishma, Dhronacharya, Karna and Dhritrashtra were present. On the contrary, Draupadi was taken to her chamber so that she could rest. Thus began a gambling game that history would never forget. As expected, the Pandavas lost all the rounds, they played owing to the sabotaged dice. Initially, they lost their wealth, livestock, estates, jewelry, etc. But later things got tense, Yudhistir gambled his entire kingdom and lost it. Things grew worse when he bet himself and all his 4 brothers one by one and lost himself and them to Duryodhana. Finally, Duryodhana decided to bet on his wife Bhanumati and Yudhistir decided to gamble Draupadi. A petrified Yudhistir closed his eyes in terror as he realized that his wife, his soul mate was no longer his. Duryodhana's mission had accomplished. He wickedly smiled and asked Dushasana to drag Draupadi from the female headquarters. The Pandavas revolted but they were silenced as they were nothing but Duryodhana's slaves. A grief-stricken and traumatized Draupadi tried her best to fight

Dushasana, but all her effort went in vain as she was dragged to the court by her hair. The moment she was thrown towards Duryodhana, she looked towards her husbands. Her head was profusely bleeding. But the five princes did not even have the guts to look their wife eye to eye, in fact, nobody in the court could except the shameless Kauravas and all bowed their heads in shame. A wronged Draupadi begged them to help her, but they were tied to Duryodhana or Hastinapur and its royalties. Duryodhana then performed the most hideous deed anyone could ever do. He asked Draupadi to sit on his thighs and ordered Dushasana to disrobe her. All heads shot up and eyes flew towards Duryodhana. They were aghast but stayed quiet. As the dreadful disrobing began, Draupadi closed her eyes and summoned Krishna. Momentarily, a divine yellow light blinded the court room. Heaps of cloth flew from the sky and covered Draupadi. Dushasana relentlessly kept pulling Draupadi's cloth, but it would not end. On the other hand, all the shawls worn by each man in the court room flew towards the divine Draupadi's feet. Their crowns broke into two halves and Dushasana's hands were burnt. Draupadi opened her eyes filled with rage ready to curse each spectator who silently witnessed her humiliation. Before she could utter a single syllable, a petrified Gandhari and distraught Kunti entered the court room. Gandhari begged Draupadi to not curse her husband and her sons. Draupadi's eyes struck up as she stared at the queen of Hastinapur. She could not believe her ears. Kunti too was taken aback and confronted her sister-in-law. She then went to console a shattered Draupadi. Gandhari then asked her husband to fulfil any wish that Draupadi asked for and a relieved Dhritrashtra agreed to do so. Draupadi looked at the entire court room and glanced at each person who had tormented her. She then saw all her five husbands sitting on the ground with their heads bowing down. She asked Dhritrashtra to release all her husbands and give them back their weapons and authority which was snatched from them deceitfully. Duryodhana on the contrary was reluctant to do so. He asked Shakuni to speak up. So, the evil Shakuni went to Dhritrashtra and whispered something in his ears to which the timid king agreed readily. He then said that Pandavas would be released but for that they would have to go on an exile for 12 years and stay in anonymity for 1 year. In that 1 year, if the Kauravas were to locate them, then the Pandavas would have to repeat the entire process. The Pandavas had no choice but to agree to the same. Duryodhana them smirked and knew what his uncle had in mind. Draupadi then left the court and went to Indraprastha. But her husbands stayed back. They vowed to avenge Draupadi's insult and claim their rights as soon as they returned. Bheem took an oath to break Duryodhana's thigh and rip off Dushasana's hand. He swore to make sure that Draupadi was bathed in Dushana's blood. Lastly, Bheem promised to kill all the hundred Kauravas. The five brothers joined hands and said that once their punishment was over, history would witness one of the most brutal battles anybody has ever seen, and it would be called 'Mahabharat'. Having said that, they marched out of the court and headed towards Indraprastha.

Upon reaching Indraprastha, the Pandavas got to know that Draupadi had locked herself in her chamber and refused to come out. No amount of legitimate force used by the Pandavas could break open that door. So, Krishna was summoned. A disappointed Krishna refused to speak to the Pandavas until Draupadi forgave them. As soon as Krishna knocked on the door twice and called out Draupadi's name, the doors flung open. All the drapes were closed, and the room sunk in darkness. Draupadi sat in one corner, an incessant river of tears shed from her eyes. Krishna went and sat next to his friend and wiped her tears. He told Draupadi that the people who had wronged her would be punished in such a horrific way that even after centuries, nobody would even think of doing such a disgusting act. However, now, all Draupadi had to do was believe in her five husbands and stay calm. Krishna then told her the grueling oaths taken by her husbands. Draupadi then hesitantly got up and went to the court room where the Pandavas and Subhadra were present. She went and announced that she would forgive the Pandavas. However, she wouldn't tie her hair before she washes it with Dushasana's blood. To this all the five brothers agreed. They then packed their belongings and headed towards the forest. Meanwhile, Subhadra was sent to Dwarka and Krishna promised to take care of his sister and his to be nephew. On the other hand, all five of Draupadi's sons headed to

Panchal and stayed with their maternal grandfather. As the Pandavas were about to exit the gates of Indraprastha, they saw Duryodhana, Shakuni and Dushasana entering Indraprastha in their chariot. They took down the flag of the Pandavas and unfurled their royal flag. As the Pandavas looked at their cousins, their eyes were filled with rage, and they made up their mind to make it all right once they returned. Having thought of that, they ventured deep into the woods.

The Exile

By the end of a few weeks, the Pandavas had built a small yet cozy hut for themselves. One afternoon, Sahadev went to bring water from the nearby pond. Suddenly, he started shouting for help, Nakul rushed towards the pond. Momentarily, he too was heard screaming. On hearing so, both Bheem and Arjun headed towards the lake. Hours passed by, but none of them returned. Draupadi became restless and asked Yudhistir to go and check. Upon reaching the bank, all Yudhistir could see was all his brothers lying dead surrounded by an uncanny mist. Before Yudhistir could grieve the loss of his brothers, a voice came from nowhere. It asked Yudhistir to answer his question correctly and if he did so then he would revive any one of his brothers. The question was to differentiate between death and life. Yudhistir then said that death and life are nothing but the entry and exit of an eternal soul. On hearing this, the voice said that it was pleased and asked Yudhistir which brother would he like to revive. A perplexed and traumatized Yudhistir looked at all his brothers. He then said that Nakul should be revived. Having said so, the voice asked Yudhistir the reason behind choosing Nakul and not Bheem and Arjun who could help him win the future war. Yudhistir then said that he loved all his brothers equally. However, his father had two wives. The son of one of his wives is alive and that is him. But a son of his stepmother, Madri, also deserved to live. So, Nakul should be revived. Suddenly, a beam of light emerged and Dharmaraj appeared in front of Yudhistir. He said that he had come to test Yudhistir and was pleased by his sense of judgement and rationality. He then revived all his four brothers and blessed them with victory and happiness in life.

The Pandavas decided to utilize the 12 years they had gotten to improve their warrior skills and increase their knowledge regarding warfare. Nakul and Sahadev decided to wander into the woods and gain extensive knowledge about herbal plants and their medicinal properties so that they could use the same to cure their wounded soldiers during the war. Bheem went on to summon Lord Hanuman and learn ways to tackle his enemies. Draupadi and Yudhistir stayed back in their hut and swore to satiate every sage that approached their household and thereby gain their blessings and goodwill. Finally, Arjun decided to meditate and summon Lord Mahadev as he was the best archer in the whole universe. Years went by, all five brothers and Draupadi were successfully accomplishing their tasks. After a stretch of 11 years, they had achieved their goal. Nakul and Sahadev had acquired various rare herbs,

Bheem had not only learnt wrestling tips but also, he understood the importance of planning and retaining his calm. Arjun gained the Pashupatastra from Lord Mahadev, a rare weapon that could slay any demon on earth. Draupadi and Yudhistir had served over 100 sages. By the end of the 12th year, the Pandavas were ready to enter anonymity. The day when their exile was about to end, the Pandavas had chalked out their entire plan. However, a final hurdle awaited them. Duryodhana along with his brother-in-law, Jayadratha and uncle, Shakuni decided to abduct Draupadi thereby ending their anonymity before it could even start. While all the Pandavas were busy doing their chores, Draupadi was cooking the afternoon meal. Suddenly, she saw Jayadratha. Unaware of his evil intentions, Draupadi was pleased to see him and asked the reason behind his sudden visit. Jayadratha cooked up a story and asked for a glass of water. As soon as the queen came out of her hut, Jayadratha summoned his charioteer and forcefully abducted Draupadi. Fortunately, all the five Pandavas saw him taking away their wife and rushed to her rescue. They captured Jayadratha and decided to shave his head off as a punishment for his misdeed. A humiliated Jayadratha swore to take revenge. With this, the Pandavas entered anonymity.

Months passed by and Duryodhana kept searching for the Pandavas, but all his efforts went in vain. Meanwhile, the Pandavas and Draupadi disguised themselves and went to Matsyanagar. They took up a fake identity. Yudhistir became King Virat's minister.

Draupadi became Queen Sunaina's hairdresser. Bheem was the royal chef. Nakul dealt with the horses and Sahadev looked after the cows. Arjun became princess Uttara's dance teacher. Everything went smoothly and within a month the Pandavas would be free. However, everything went awry when Kichak, Queen Sunaina's brother decoded Draupadi's truth. He asked Draupadi to meet him in his chamber if she wanted her secret to be kept hidden. Draupadi informed Bheem about Kichak's unacceptable behavior and Bheem decided to assassinate Kichak. As soon as the news of Kichak's death reached Hastinapur, Duryodhana very well knew that the Pandavas were in Matsyanagar because someone as powerful as Kichak could only be killed by Bheem. So, one day before the end of the anonymity, Duryodhana set out with his army to capture the Pandavas. However, before he could get hold of them, the sunset marked the end of the day. However, a cunning Duryodhana went up to his father and falsely claimed that he had found the Pandavas before sunset and therefore they should repeat their punishment. This time, the Pandavas refused to abide by Dhritrashtra's order. They stood their stance and decided to wage a war. This marked the beginning of the Mahabharata.

The Beginning of the End

Before the disastrous war could commence, Krishna tried to opt for a peaceful path one last time. He approached the authorities of Hastinapur and asked them to give Pandavas their share and seek forgiveness from Draupadi. However, an egoistic Duryodhana humiliated Krishna and asked him to leave the premises at once. Krishna now knew that war was the only ultimatum.

With this, the date and timing of the war were decided. Both the Pandavas and Kauravas reached out to their allies and asked for their respective armies. However, Dwarka got intertwined in between both the nemesis. While Krishna was Kunti's nephew, Duryodhana was Balram's favorite student. As a result, Krishna announced that on one hand was his humungous army and on the other was an armless Krishna himself. Well, the Pandavas chose Krishna while Duryodhana chose his army.

Soon after, the Pandavas reunited with their sons and informed them about the war. To their surprise, all their sons pledged to avenge their mother and fight till their last breath. With Krishna's blessings, Abhimanyu, Arjun and Subhadra's son married Uttara, Virat, and Sunaina's daughter. With this. The Pandavas also got economical and military support from Matsya Nagar.

Everything was set. However, Krishna knew that it would be difficult to win the war if Karna, Duryodhana's friend, was not defeated. And for that to take place, it was important to get rid of his golden armor and earrings. Karna had committed many sins in his life. Guilt-ridden, he would perform heartly donations in the hope of reducing some amount of his regret. One afternoon, Indradev approached Karna disguised as a sage and asked for his armor and earrings. Karna then cut off his earrings and tore the golden shield apart and gave it to the sage. However, upon tearing his shield, his chest started bleeding profusely and he took help from Nakul and Sahadev. Since, Karna had asked for their help before the war, they aided him. As a result of which Karna was now obliged to both the Pandava brothers and swore to return their favor. Late that evening, Kunti approached Karna and revealed a startling fact. To this Karna made Kunti a promise that he abided by till his last breath.

Soon after, the war began. All the armies assembled in Kurukshetra. However, seeing his mentor, grandfather, and all elders on the other side. Arjun went cold feet and dropped his weapons. Upon witnessing Arjun's dilemma, Krishna, his charioteer, gave him a preaching that the entire world would remember as Bhagavad Gita.

Bhagavad Gita

Krishna's lifetime preachings and ideals recorded in one book that has influenced zillions of people over time.

The Bhagavat Gita, often referred to as the Gita, is a 700 verse Hindu scripture that is a major part of the epic Mahabharata. The Gita is a set framework of a dialogue between Pandava prince, Arjuna and his guide and charioteer Krishna. At the start of the Dharma Yudha between the Pandavas and Kauravas, Arjuna, a great warrior, was filled with moral dilemma and despair about the violence and death the war would cause in the battle against his own kin. He seeks Krishna's counsel, whose answers constitute the holy book, Gita. Krishna encourages Arjuna to uphold his duty through selfless action.

Love: Lord Krishna said that even Brahma could be achieved with love. Sages have said that love opens all the doors. We make enemies from emotions like hate, anger, vengeance and other such feelings. People must understand that we can win people to our sides by spreading love and losing such negative emotions.

'Do everything you have to,

But not with greed,

Not with ego,

Not with envy,

But love, compassion, humility, and devotion'

War: Shri Krishna gave clarity to the thought that confused a person whether they should fight with their relatives, teachers, and friends. He said fight for the sake of duty, treating alike happiness and distress. If one tries to fulfil his/her responsibility in this way, one will never incur sin.

'If you don't fight for what you want,

Don't cry for what you lost.'

Death: Lord Krishna said that the soul transfers from one body to another. Unlike the body the soul is immortal and never dies. It is not perishable under any circumstances.

'The soul migrates from body to body,

Weapons cannot cleave it,

Nor fire consume it,

Nor water drenches it,

Nor wind dries it.'

Karma: Krishna said that whatever deeds a person does, he/she has to face the consequences

according to that. He said after explaining the depth of all the shlokas this is the only truth of the universe.

'You have the right to work,

But not to fruit the work.

You should never engage in an action for the sake of reward'

A few shlokas along with their translations are as follows:

नवानि गृह्णाति नरोऽपराणि |

तथा शरीराणि विहाय जीर्णा

न्यन्यानि संयाति नवानि देही ||

(Chapter 2, Verse 2)

As a person sheds worn-out garments and wears new ones, likewise, at the time of death, the soul casts off its worn-out body and enters a new one.

आपूर्यमाणमचलप्रतिष्ठं

समुद्रमाप: प्रविशन्ति यद्वत् |

तद्वत्कामा यं प्रविशन्ति सर्वे

स शान्तिमाप्नोति न कामकामी ॥

(Chapter 2, Verse 70)

Just as the ocean remains undisturbed by the incessant flow of waters from rivers merging into it, likewise the sage who is unmoved despite the flow of desirable objects all around him attains peace, and not the person who strives to satisfy desires.

त्रिविधं नरकस्येदं द्वारं नाशनमात्मनः |

कामः क्रोधस्तथा लोभस्तस्मादेतत्त्रयं त्यजेत् ॥

(Chapter 16, Verse 21)

There are three gates leading to the hell of self-destruction for the soul — lust, anger, and greed. Therefore, all should abandon these three.

इन्द्रियाणि पराण्याहुरिन्द्रियेभ्यः परं मनः |

मनसस्तु परा बुद्धिर्यो बुद्धेः परतस्तु सः ॥

(Chapter 3, Verse 42)

The senses are superior to the gross body, and superior to the senses is the mind. Beyond the mind is the intellect, and even beyond the intellect is the soul.

With this, Arjun realised that it was Krishna who won or lost the battled. It was Krishna who was fighting. It was Krishna who was dying. Having accepted reality. Arjun upheld his weapon and asked his elder brother to commence the war and seek justice. With this the Mahabharata began.

The War

On the first day of war, the Pandavas faced a fierce upheaval, Uttar, Virat and Sunaina's son gave up his life while protecting Yudhistir and soon afterwards, Virat also died. But by the 2nd day, the Pandavas were back in the game and took their revenge.

A brutal battle continued till the 9th day. By then Bhishma, advised the Pandavas to bring Shikhandi into the play. Or else, they would soon lose. Bhishma had promised Shikhandi (an incarnation of Amba) that he would surrender his weapons the day she entered the battlefield. However, being a woman, she was not allowed to enter the war premises. So, a determined Shikhandi did a hardcore penance for 1 week and asked god to change her gender for merely 24 hours. On the 10th day of the war, Shikhandi entered the war and seeing her Bhishma threw his weapons. Arjun then fired 100 arrows on his grandsire, and he was put on a bed of arrows. With this Dronacharya became the commanding officer. Since Bhishma could decide his death, he decided to watch the complete war and see the Pandavas emerge victorious before he retired from the world.

On the 13th day of the war, the Pandavas were welcomed with both a good and bad news. One one hand they got to know that Uttara was pregnant with Abhimanyu's child. While out on the battlefield, the

Pandavas had created a chakravyuh (a trap that was not easy to break). While the Kauravas created a deviation for Krishna and Arjun, they trapped a huge chunk of the Pandava army. As a result of which, the other four Pandavas had no option but to break the chakravyuh. The problem was that no one apart from Arjun knew how to do so and he was sent away. Abhimanyu then claimed that he knew how to do so. He had learnt how to break into the chakravyuh when he was in his mother's womb. However, before he could get to know how to get out of it, Subhadra fell asleep. But the Pandavas were reluctant to send him into a death trap. After a lot of debating, it was decided that Abhimanyu would break into the trap and the Pandavas would follow him. However, little did they know that a cunning ploy awaited them. On entering the centre of the strategic forming, they found Jayadratha. He fired a weapon that could imprison anybody on Earth except Arjun. As a result of this all the Pandavas were held captive and they watched their nephew being killed brutally Infront of their eyes. The next day Arjun swore revenge. He took an oath that he would kill Jayadratha before sunset oresle set himself on fire. A coward Jayadratha hid in his tent throughout the day. Then Krishna too got into foul play. He used his weapon to cover the sun making the Kauravas feel that it was sunset. Jayadratha then emerged from his tent and as soon as he did, Krishna revealed his treachery. Jayadratha then revealed his boon. He said that whoever would make his head fall on the ground would be reduced to ashes. Arjun then smirked and fired his arrow which beheaded Jayadratha and took his head all the way to his mentor who gave him the boon. Jayadratha's head then fell on his guru's lap and the sage got up in aghast and was immediately reduced to ashes.

The next day, Dhrishtadyum killed Dronacharya and Karna killed Bheem's son, Ghatotkach. By the 16th day, Bheem had assassinated 98 of the Kauravas. Only Dushasana and Duryodhana were left. However, on the 16th day, Dushasana was killed too. Bheem ripped his arms out and tore his chest apart. Then he called Draupadi to the war field and bathed her hair with Dushasana's blood and tied it. With this, Bheem fulfilled his promise to his wife. The 17th day marked Karna's death. All of a sudden, Karna's chariot broke, and he knelt down to mend it. Suddenly. Parshuram's curse came into play and Arjun fired an arrow that hit Karna's neck. A disheartened Kunti rushed to the battlefield and held Karna on her lap. She then narrated a tale from her past. When she had gotten the boon from Rishi Durvasa of bearing a child from whichever god she wanted, Kunti wanted to test its efficacy. So, she summoned the Sun god and got Karna. However, she was very young and unmarried and that child would tarnish her reputation. So, she put Karna in a basket and put it in a river. That basket then reached Karna's foster parents, Radha, and Adhiratha (Bhishma's charioteer) and they decided to raise Karna. That evening Kunti had revealed this secret to Karna, and he promised Kunti that out of her 6 sons, 5 would always remain alive. Pandavas bowed down their head and performed Karna's last rites.

That night, Duryodhana asked his mother to open her blindfold. Upon doing so, she could use power of her devotion to make Duryodhana's body as strong as iron. Duryodhana then took of his clothes behind a tree. Krishna then told him to at least wrap a maple leaf around his private parts oresle his mother would faint due to disgust. Duryodhana agreed to do so. Well, as Krishna had planned Duryodhana's entire body became as strong as iron except his thighs which were also covered by the maple leaf. The following day, Bheem decoded the same and hit Duryodhana on his thigh and broke it. With this, Duryodhana was on the verge of dying. He then called Ashwathama and asked him to kill the Pandavas and their entire lineage. Ashwathama promised to complete his friend's last wish and Duryodhana died. Shakuni was too killed by Sahadev. The Pandavas had won but the real battle was still left.

On the 18th day, Ashwathama killed Dhrishtadyum and the five sons of the Pandavas while they were asleep. He then fired his Brahmastra on Uttara's womb to kill her unborn child. Krishna was enraged seeing such a heartless deal. He cursed Ashwathama to live till eternity but all this while he would fall prey to the worst kind of diseases that would evolve with time. Krishna along with the Pandavas rushed to Uttara's tent. Krishna then used all his good deeds to revive

Uttara's womb. He then named her to be son Parakshit (one who was tested before birth).

The Pandavas then went to Hastinapur to claim the throne. Dhritrashtra decided to avenge the death of his sons by embracing Bheem to his death. Bur before Bheem could hug his uncle, Krishna pulled him back and put a statue near the king. Dhritrashtra then crushed the wooden statue to pieces. He realised his mistake and asked for forgiveness from the Pandavas. With this, the Pandavas won the battle and got their rights. However, it all came at a huge cost.

Gandhari's Curse

Yudhistir was crowned as the king of Hastinapur. However, Gandhari, mother of the Kauravas had lost all her 100 sons and was filled with vengeance, hatred, and anger. She held Krishna responsible for the death of all her sons and the destruction of the Kuru dynasty. She felt that Krishna had provoked the Pandavas to wage a war against the Kauravas and he used treachery to get her sons killed. Therefore, she cursed Krishna to beget the same amount of pain she had tolerated. Gandhari's curse was, that alike her Krishna would have to helplessly witness his entire kin fight amongst each other till the time of their death. They would brutally murder each other for materialistic provisions and Krishna would be nothing but a traumatised spectator.

A tear rolled down Krishna's eyes as he willingly accepted the curse and smiled his way back.

Krishna's Death

Upon reaching Dwarka, Krishna realized that Gandhari's curse had taken effect. All his heirs were fighting amongst each other to gain control over the prestigious throne of Dwarka. His children were ready to kill their half-brothers if that was the price for obtaining the throne and kingship. They drew diabolical plans and mercilessly executed their kinsmen. Amidst this chaotic situation, bloodshed bestowed its authority. A tear rolled down Krishna's eye as he saw his entire kin get reduced to ashes in front of him. Within a year, Krishna sorrowfully cremated all his sons. He pondered upon the fact that fate and time are both so unpredictable, a few months ago all his sons were fighting for a materialistic thing and now they all were dead and that embellishment was isolated and a property of none. Krishna now knew that it was time for him to renounce the world. He bid adieu to his remaining family and his citizens and went to meet Radha for one last time. Radha, the love of Krishna's life, a lady with whom Krishna did not share any marital bond yet loved her immensely after all she was an incarnation of the supreme Goddess Lakshmi herself. As Krishna embraced Radha for one last time, he did not need to utter a single word because Radha understood it all. She silently placed her head on his shoulder and asked him to play the flute. As the melodious tune of the instrument entered her head, she closed her eyes forever. Krishna lay emotionless, placing Radha's corpse on his lap and clinging onto it throughout the night. He reminded himself of Radha's oath in which she proclaimed that she would die before Krishna could. After performing Radha's last rites, he broke his flute saying that it was a symbol of his pure love for his beloved Radha. Now that she had left him forever, his flute was of no use. The following day, he sat near a bush, nostalgically reminiscing his entire life. He closed his eyes as an arrow came out the bush and pierced the lotus present on his feet. Krishna uttered a painful cry and appeared from the bushes a hunter named Jara. Upon introducing himself, he joint both his hands and fell down on the ground. An incessant river of guilt flowed from his eyes. He said that he saw Krishna's feet gleaming from far away and mistakenly assumed it to be a deer and shot his arrow. Krishna forgave him and loudly pronounced Radha's name twice as life slowly ebbed away from him. On the other hand, huge waves engulfed the extravagant city of Dwarka as it got submerged in the water forever. With Krishna death, Kali Yuga began with a cataclysm on Earth.

Some believe that Jara was a re-incarnation of Bali, the Vanar King of Kishkindha who was killed by Ram in the Treta Yuga so that Sugriv could be crowned as the King. However, Ram had shot an arrow from behind the bushes which was targeted at Bali's back. This was against the Kshatriya principles as not only did Ram kill an enemy from the back but also legally, he was not indulged in the fight either. Ram was aware of the sin he had committed and asked Bali for forgiveness. On the contrary, a furious Bali who was dying told Ram that his soul wanted revenge not a peaceful coherence. Therefore, Ram acknowledged and accepted his last wish and said that Bali would take a rebirth as Jara and kill his 8th Avatar Krishna in the Dvapara Yuga. By doing this he could take his 'revenge'. Bali readily agreed to this and lay dead.

By taking these human avatars such as that of Lord Krishna and Lord Rama, Lord Narayan tries to signify the fact that be it god or anyone else, they have to face hardships in their life. They would have to lament over their losses and endure the pain of losing or getting separated from their loved ones. In fact even God cried for love. Life will not always be a bed of roses. Mostly, it will be a mountain of thorns and in order to reach the top, one will have to cross all the obstacles. Amidst all this hardship, finding the correct friends, soulmate and mentors is what will make it a memorable journey. In today's world, adharma has reached its peak. In such a scenario, never ever giving up one's pure beliefs is what will save everyone. It does not take even a second to deviate from the correct path but sticking onto it throughout one's life is what requires a great deal of effort, sacrifice and motivation. Alongside, lord Krishna gave the world the secret to live life, a human manual, the Bhagavad Gita. He answered all questions in the world in that one dictation implementing it is what is now human's duty.

11. Buddha Avatar

During 563 B.C., in Lumbini, King Suddhodana and Queen Maya bore a son named Siddharth. However, due to severe complications in her pregnancy, Queen Maya passed away when Prince Siddharth was a merely an infant. Therefore, Queen Gautami, King Suddhodana's second wife stepped into the role of a mother and pledged to foster Siddharth and impart good values in him. As per the Hindu traditions, an astrologer was called upon to predict the little prince's future. After precisely analyzing Siddharth's birth chart, he announced that if the prince would be kept aloof from the miseries and reality of the world outside the palace, he would turn out to be a notable emperor. On the flip side, if the aforementioned did not happen, he would renounce the world and become a memorable and respectable saint. Since then, King Suddhodana made sure that Siddharth wouldn't leave the royal premises at any cost.

Therefore, years passed by, Siddharth grew up to be a charismatic prince. At the age of 16, he married Princess Yashodhara. They had a son named Rahul.

Siddharth spent 25 years of his life as befitted royalty. However, one day when he went out for hunting, he saw an old man, a sick man and lastly a dead man. Upon seeing this grief-stricken truth of life, Siddharth went back to his palace and decided to gain enlightenment regarding the cyclicity of life and the inevitability of death. He left his family and passed his throne to his immature son and embarked on his knowledgeable journey.

Siddharth kept wandering for 7 years in search for a place where he could gain wisdom. Finally, he sat under the Peepal tree and meditated consistently for 6 years. Lastly, he had accomplished his mission. Since then that tree was known as the 'Bodhi tree' and Siddharth was renamed as 'Gautam Buddha'.

Buddha is a Sanskrit word which literally means 'the awakened one'. On the other hand, Siddharth's mother's name was Gautami. Therefore, he was referred to as Gautam Buddha. He remained unaffected by the transit nature of life. He had broken himself free from all the vices of the world. His life was solely dedicated for the benefit and upliftment of mankind and therefore, we praise his sacrifice by considering him as the ninth avatar of Lord Vishnu.

Buddha then travelled to various places and preached his teachings to all. He left manuscripts for the development of mankind. All the people who worshipped him and his ideals related to non-violence were known as Buddhists.

The 4 foremost teachings of Buddha are prevalent and rampant in our society as the 'Four Notable Truths'. They are as follows:

- **All beings experience pain and misery (dukkha) during their lifetime**: *"Birth is pain, old age is pain, sickness is pain, death is pain; sorrow, grief and anxiety are pain. Contact with the unpleasant is pain. Separating from the pleasant is pain. Not getting what one wants is pain. In short, the five assemblies of mind and matter that are subjected to attachment are pain."*

- **The origin (samudaya) of pain and misery is due to a specific cause**: *"It is the desire that leads to rebirth, accompanied by pleasure and passion, seeking pleasure here and there; that is, the desire for pleasures, the desire for existence, the desire for non-existence."*

- **The cessation (nirodha) of pain and misery can be achieved as follows**: *"With the complete non-passion and cessation of this very desire, with its abandonment and renunciation, with its liberation and detachment from it."*

- **The method we must follow to stop pain and misery is that of the Noble Eightfold Path.**

These truths do not exist in external things such as grass, wood and stones; they do exist though, in our body, which is composed of material elements and mental elements, such as consciousness and perception. As the Buddha says, **"In this body with its perception and consciousness I declare the world of pain, the origin, the cessation, and the practice that leads to its cessation."**

Noble Eightfold Path (a set of conceptual and psychological ideas for the development of the state of mind) includes right understanding, thought, speech, action, livelihood, mindfulness, concentration and practices.

Tale 1:

*One day, an old and fragile lady named Kisa Gotami went crying to Gautam Buddha. She said that her son departed from the world this morning and she wanted Gautam Buddha to revive his son. Buddha agreed to fulfil the poor lady's demand. However, he presented a condition before her. He said that she had to collect mustard seeds from someone's house where none of their ancestors have died. Kisa Gotami readily agreed and relentlessly went to each house reiterating the Buddha's demand. However, everywhere she went she was either laughed upon or looked at with a pitiful glance. Finally, Kisa Gotami gave up and sat in front of her hut. A few meters ahead, she saw a chandelier flickering and momentarily it stopped glowing. Instantly she understood what Buddha was trying to teach her. She realized that one's life is alike the chandelier. Once it starts to flicker, we know that it will stop working within a few minutes and when it does not shine, we know that it is broken and nothing can be done to reignite it. One can only replace it with a new one. She went to the Buddha next day and thanked him for teaching her an unforgettable epistemology of life. Buddha then told all his disciples that **<u>death is a leveler and its approach towards everyone's life is unbiased and equal.</u>***

Tale 2:

*One day, while Buddha addressed his disciples, he said that one should always maintain their calm in all adverse and humiliating situations. Suddenly, a student accused Buddha by stating that he only knew how to preach and impart tons of education. However, he himself didn't know how to practice them in his own life. He abused Buddha, spat upon him and disregarded his penance. But all this while, Buddha remained quiet and did not punish the student. The following morning when the student realized his sin of mortifying an idyllic figure like the Buddha, he went in order to seek forgiveness. Amusingly, the Buddha failed to recognize him and asked him to introduce himself. The student was awestruck and said that he had embarrassed him by questioning his learning the day before and then asked him how he could possibly forget such a disgrace within a few hours. Buddha then smiled and replied that he had **never given much importance to all the unfortunate events that have had occurred in the past.**__*

Buddha summarized the principle of life as follows:

"The secret of health for both mind and body is not to mourn for the past, nor to worry about the future, but to live the present moment wisely and earnestly."

In order to seek all answers in life and gain enlightenment, it is important to renounce the worldly pleasures. By taking the Buddha Avatar, Lord Vishnu symbolizes the fact that as long as a human is affected by the world in which he/she lives, he/she cannot be enlightened. This is because the world is mortal. It is meant to end one day. Grieving about one's losses and procrastinating about what the future holds will only bring pain. Admitting the fact that life is transitional and the soul is what stays till eternity is what will make someone learned. Worldly pain can be only neglected in one way that is breaking ties from it. This is exactly what the Buddha avatar did and taught.

12. Kalki Avatar

The Kalki Avatar is the tenth and last avatar of Lord Vishnu which has not been born yet. Some puranas say that it will take place approximately 4 lakh years later (*according to the Vikram Samvat; Hindi Calendar*) when the Kala Yug will end. This avatar will appear during the darkest period of human history when values degenerate like never before. We are currently in the 5121st year (*according to the Vikram Samvat*) of Kala Yug and dharma has already degraded primarily. With righteousness getting exploited at such an alarming rate, very soon adharma will prevail. A few scriptures record Lord Kalki's appearance as a broad-shouldered youth wearing armor, carrying a gleaming sword, and riding a white colored horse named Devadatta. With an aggressive look on his face, he charges upon the evils who question mankind's existence.

13. Conclusion

The ten avatars of Lord Vishnu also can be interpreted in yet another way. A closer glance at them will reveal the fact that they represent the theory of evolution.

- Matsya - fish (Paleozoic era)
- Kachhap - amphibious tortoise (Mesozoic era)
- Varaha - boar (Cenozoic era)
- Narasimha - man-lion, the last animal and semi-human avatar (Cenozoic era)
- Vamana - growing dwarf and first step towards the human form
- Parasurama - an early man who started using primitive weapons like Axe
- Rama - an ideal hero, physically perfect, befriends a speaking vanara deity Hanuman
- Krishna - Vishnu incarnating as a god
- Buddha - the founder of Buddhism, an enlightened man

- Kalki - the next step of the evolution, yet to happen, the savior

These 10 avatars symbolize the evolution from fish (water breeding animals) to humans (reaching the stage of enlightenment).

At this point it is necessary to answer one question which might be there in everyone's mind. At the end of the day, who is Vishnu?

Vishnu – the epitome of righteousness, the embodiment of perseverance, the faith of millions of people, the ideal husband, the savior of the world. In fact, it is impossible to define Vishnu. His existence is far beyond and divine than one can imagine. In various Upanishads, three words come hand in hand with Vishnu's name - omnipresent, omnipotent, and omniscient. It means one who is present everywhere, is the most powerful being and knows everything.

Vishnu is that supreme entity who is always present in everyone's conscience. He is the 'param-atma', origin of everything, everyone. Some might call him Allah while others may refer to him as Christ. However, there is this one power – a source of unimaginable energy which cannot be explained through any possible scientific means. That is Vishnu.

As mentioned previously, interpreting all the ten avatars of Lord Vishnu is not possible. Had that been feasible, everyone could have been Vishnu. The main purpose of all the avatars was to teach people how to live life. As Darwen stated, evolution is a process of selection of the best. However, channeling the thought process of humans, teaching them to utilize their true potential and showing them the ideal way of living life is what Lord Vishnu taught through those ten incarnations. They were not only meant to liberate the world from the crisis in which they were stuck. In fact it was to teach something to the generations that followed. This is sadly something that today's people have forgotten. However, it's never late to rectify one's mistake. By taking these avatars, lord Vishnu showcased 10 ways of living one's life. Interestingly, the last and most crucial one is yet to be unraveled.

www.ingramcontent.com/pod-product-compliance
Lightning Source LLC
LaVergne TN
LVHW041611070526
838199LV00052B/3091